Resilience: Aging with Vision, Hope and Courage in a Time of Crisis

Finding Our Way Together

The *Resilience* Series

Resilience: Aging with Vision, Hope and Courage in a Time of Crisis

Finding Our Way Together

John Robinson

CHANGEMAKERS
BOOKS

Winchester, UK
Washington, USA

JOHN HUNT PUBLISHING

First published by Changemakers Books, 2020
Changemakers Books is an imprint of John Hunt Publishing Ltd., No. 3 East Street,
Alresford, Hampshire SO24 9EE, UK
office@jhpbooks.com
www.johnhuntpublishing.com
www.changemakers-books.com

For distributor details and how to order please visit the 'Ordering' section on our website.

Text copyright: John Robinson 2020

ISBN: 978 1 78904 685 4
978 1 78904 686 1 (ebook)
Library of Congress Control Number: 2020937193

A CIP catalogue record for this book is available from the British Library.

Design: Stuart Davies

UK: Printed and bound by CPI Group (UK) Ltd, Croydon, CR0 4YY
Printed in North America by CPI GPS partners

We operate a distinctive and ethical publishing philosophy in
all areas of our business, from our global network of authors to
production and worldwide distribution.

Contents

Previous Books

Death of a Hero, Birth of the Soul: Answering the Call
of Midlife
1571780432
But Where Is God? Psychotherapy and the Religious Search
1560725046
Ordinary Enlightenment: Experiencing God's Presence in
Everyday Life
0871592614
Finding Heaven Here
1846941566
The Three Secrets of Aging: A Radical Guide
1780990408
Bedtime Stories for Elders: What Fairy Tales Can Teach Us
About the New Aging
1780993539
What Aging Men Want: The Odyssey as a Parable
of Male Aging
1780999814
Breakthrough
1785350924
The Divine Human: The Final Transformation of Sacred Aging
1780992365
Mystical Activism: Transforming a World in Crisis
1789044188

A man stands among the redwoods.
He knows them as his ancestors – ancient, noble, timeless, calm, conscious.
Listening and comprehending, he gathers wisdom and strength for the coming storm.

Foreword

"What can we do to help?"

In a time of crisis – such as the 2020 Covid-19 pandemic – we all have a natural impulse to help our neighbors. John Hunt, founder of John Hunt Publishing, asked this question of our company, and then offered a suggestion. He proposed producing a series of short books written by experts offering practical, emotional, and spiritual skills to help people survive in the midst of a crisis.

To reach people when they need it most, John wanted to accomplish this in forty days. Bear in mind, the normal process of bringing a book from concept to market takes at least eighteen months. As publisher of the JHP imprint Changemakers Books, I volunteered to execute this audacious plan. My imprint publishes books about personal and social transformation, and I already knew many authors with exactly the kinds of expertise we needed. That's how the *Resilience* series was born.

I was overwhelmed by my authors' responses. Ten of them immediately said yes and agreed to the impossible deadline. The book you hold in your hands is the result of this intensive, collaborative effort. On behalf of John, myself, the authors and production team, our intention for you is that you take to heart the skills and techniques offered to you in this these pages. Master them. Make yourself stronger. Share your newfound resilience with those around you. Together, we can not only survive, but learn how to thrive in tough times. By so doing, we can find our way to a better future.

Tim Ward
Publisher, Changemakers Books
May 1, 2020

Preface

May I introduce myself? I'm a retired clinical psychologist, with a second doctorate in ministry, an ordained interfaith minister, and a writer, but I'm also a husband, father, grandfather, friend, and lifelong mystic. I've been writing and lecturing on conscious aging as a spiritual and mystical experience for over twenty-five years. Then, more recently, I came to see that a spiritual and mystical awareness of life is also critical to our survival in the rapidly escalating climate crisis, so I wrote, *Mystical Activism: Transforming a World in Crisis*. But now there's even more. As the coronavirus burst upon the scene, I realized that climate change was only one of a new "Four Horsemen of the Apocalypse." The storied marauders of old – death, plague, war and famine – had morphed into COVID-19, climate change, uncontrolled population growth, and the unraveling of modern civilization.

We are now heading into a sustained global crisis. Increasingly, I fear for the future of my family and friends, as I'm sure you fear for the future of your loved ones, and I worry for the future of the human family and life itself. This is not academic to me, it's in my awareness every day, triggered by each news report, email, telephone conversation, and article I write. I live and breathe it constantly. So do you. That's why I wrote, *Resilience: Aging with Vision, Hope and Courage in a Time of Crisis*.

A friend of mine, Kristal Parks, who is a biologist and Earth activist with a masters in Peace, Justice and Social Transformation, recently shared,

I start with the awareness that the Earth is a living, dynamic organism. And like all living things, seeks to rid itself of anything harmful and threatening to its wellbeing. There is nothing more threatening to Mother Earth than us, we human beings. I wish to suggest that the coronavirus and other very threatening viruses (like Ebola and the

Swine flu virus), are the Earth's way of trying to rid herself of the parasite that is killing her... US! These viruses are canaries in the mine shaft. And perhaps they are more friend than foe.

I don't think pandemics will end until we stop what we are doing that is destroying the Earth, our home. So besides taking precautions to protect ourselves (wash our hands, cough into a Kleenex, etc.), I suggest we also take a very deep look at what is making Mother Earth mad as hell, and do all we can to change that. So, when things settle down and kids go back to school and restaurants open again, I hope we won't go back to life "as usual," doing the same old, same old stuff that is driving ourselves, and all life, to extinction. Let's listen to the clarion call of the sentinel Coronavirus and make all the changes we need to. Now.

At a larger level, Kristal is describing "Creation in Crisis," a toxic brew of global pandemics, climate disruption, population explosion, the unraveling of modern civilization, all of which portend the ending of life as we know it. While this Gaia-like hypothesis may be as much a metaphor as testable reality, it rings true to me. Creation is in trouble and we are the cause. It is in this context that we must take stock and make "all the changes we need to."

Some people say that they aren't too concerned about all this, that it's either exaggerated or beyond control, so why worry. They party on the Titanic. Others turn to distractions like television and the Internet, or the numbing effects of alcohol, drugs, gambling, busyness, or related addictions, to mute their emotional distress. But as we all know, that changes nothing except our own awareness, growth and resilience. Sadly, the truth is that these Four Horsemen can pull the rug out from under anyone at any time, no matter who you are, where you live, what you believe, or how much money you have. We must resist barricading ourselves in denial and instead open heart, mind and soul to the possibilities of personal and global transformation. This book may not be what you expected but it may be what you need.

This is a frightening time. Even as I write this, I feel the surreal unreality, fear and isolation of mandatory coronavirus lockdown. Whether it ends sooner or later, our mounting problems will not pass quickly – we must face our fears together, and they are many.

- I know you are scared. I am, too.
- I know you fear being infected with the coronavirus. I do, too.
- I know you often feel helplessness and despair reading the daily news. I do, too.
- I also know that you cope with the unstoppable progression of age and its effects on your body, mind, independence, and social life. I do, too.
- I know that despite your religious beliefs, you fear the coming of death. Me, too.
- I know you worry about losing your spouse or remaining friends to illness and facing this nightmare alone. I do, too.
- I know you're afraid of running out of money in a time of failing social services. I am, too.
- I know you worry about the breakdown of social order, stability and security, I do, too.

I am 74 years old. I am writing this book for you and me and for all of us past 65 trying to survive a complicated and frightening global crisis. This is my story, too. But with thirty years as a psychotherapist and twenty-five as a writer on spirituality and aging, I have learned a lot and want to share what I hope will help all of us survive with dignity, courage and love in this rapidly crumbling world. This is the book I would want to read. I offer it to you with deepest respect.

Introduction

This book is for anyone over 65 wrestling with fear, despair, insecurity, and loneliness in this time of crisis. A blend of psychology, self-help and spirituality, it's tailored for all of us – everyday people and mature spiritual seekers – who need facts, respect, compassion, and meaningful resources to light the path ahead. Indeed, my deep respect for you, my peers, insists that this be a truthful book that does not trivialize the danger of this rapidly changing reality, yet also an inspiring one, describing the very real possibility of personal and social transformation. My emphasis is on eternal values like candor, respect, empathy, love, and understanding, and our profound potential for psychological, social and spiritual growth. We are not senile, we are mature, capable, and caring people. Like the young and middle-aged, we do not feel old on the inside, but we are deeply vulnerable. As a member of this demographic, my goal is to move us all from fear and paralysis to growth and engagement.

I am particularly focused on the emotional and spiritual needs we share. For example, I need to feel safe. I need to feel loved and wanted. I need to feel productive and inspired. I need to find meaning and purpose in my daily life. I need to feel a sense of belonging to family, friends, community and life. I need practical tools for surviving the threats around me. I need friends and family to help me cope. I need to understand my life in the larger context of human history and the spiritual significance of this time. I need to know and experience the divine for comfort and inspiration. I need to know that people will love and care for me at the end. And I need to feel that my life has been worthwhile and that I have left something positive from my sojourn here on Earth. Can you identify with these needs? Which ones do you most identify with? Can you name any I have missed? We are all in this together.

To meet these needs, *Resilience: Aging with Vision, Hope and Courage in a Time of Crisis* provides emotional guidance, survival tools, personal growth exercises, a symbolic map of our journey, and a larger understanding of this time in history. To that end, Part I highlights the transformational possibilities of aging and the gifts of maturity we have grown in our wisdom years to help us cope with the challenging realities of today's world; Part II acknowledges the overwhelming emotions we are beginning to feel, presents a practical guide for surviving them, and invites the reader to discover his or her personal gifts for healing the world; Part III explores the mystical dimension of life and a powerful mystical allegory of our shared journey from denial, fear and paralysis, to vision, hope, and courage, and in the end, the work of our souls; and Part IV addresses this unprecedented moment in history, describing its larger spiritual context and revelation of a new humanity that may come if and when we fall in love with Creation again.

You will probably find this to be an unusual book and some parts may frankly surprise you, but don't dismiss the possibilities for spiritual growth and transformation found in these pages. I have been mining insights from my work on conscious aging and spiritual transformation for decades and I want to share them with you. These unusual times require both conventional and unconventional approaches, but everything presented here has a well-established basis even if unfamiliar to you. Get ready to change your mind and your life.

Finally, read this book again and again. Read it slowly. Use it like a workbook. Explore your life with its exercises. Return to the most helpful parts to bring forth new gems of insight and action. Recognize also that we are all unique and that some topics will seem more relevant than others. No worries. Find what works! It's like a supermarket – just pick what you need at the time. Plus, you definitely won't be bored! For additional information on any particular topic, consult the list of Sources on the last page. And last but not least, realize that this book is a living experience – it will change you, your life, and your goals if you take it seriously. Please take it seriously.

Part I. Aging in a Time of Crisis

You are I have seen a lot in our lifetimes. What you may not know is that our recently extended life span has transformed aging into a new developmental stage integrating a lifetime of hard-won resilience with new psychological and spiritual growth, all in preparation for the trials ahead. If we're going to face the global nightmare swirling around us, we should start by reminding ourselves of who we are and the powerful resources we have to confront the approaching storm.

Chapter 1

Good News: We're Resilient, Brand New, and Still Growing

Before we tackle the difficult facts of this new time, I want to start with the good news: we are resilient, we are still growing, and we share our new maturity with each other and the world. We begin the journey with vision, hope and courage.

Resilience. As older men and women in the twenty-first century, we have lived through extraordinary times: *Constant Wars*: World War II, Korean War, Viet Nam War, 911, Iraq and Afghanistan Wars; *Economic Turmoil*: The Great Depression, 2008 recession, and now enormous wealth inequality; *Natural Disasters*: Earthquakes, tsunamis, tornados, hurricanes, floods, famines, and volcanic eruptions; *Technological Advances*: Television, air travel, the space exploration, computers, the Internet, artificial intelligence, speech recognition, nanotechnology, solar and wind energy, and electric cars; *Medical Discoveries*: Antibiotics, vaccines, cardiac surgeries, brain stimulation, genetic engineering, and cancer treatments; *Scientific Achievements*: genetics, nuclear power, the Big Bang, particle physics, and a new cosmology; *Social Change*: Civil Rights Movement, Women's Liberation, the assassinations of Martin Luther King and John and Robert Kennedy; *Political Change*: the arms race, cold war, Johnson's Great Society, Nixon's resignation, the fall of the Berlin Wall, Clinton's impeachment, our first African-American president, cyber warfare; *The Tumultuous Trump Presidency*; and *Iconic Events in Religion, Sports, Fashion, the Arts, Cinema* too numerous to chronicle here. In sum, we have witnessed and adapted to vast and continuous change; the very fact that we are still standing is a testament to our strength and resilience, traits that will serve us again in the coming planetary upheaval. We are survivors.

The New Aging. Adding to the depth of our resilience, however, is another extraordinary resource – our recently-extended longevity. For nearly all of recorded history, only one person in ten could hope to reach 65 years of age. When Thomas Jefferson was around, half the population in America was under the age of 16. The average life span in 1900 was 45. With the medical and dietary advances in the last one hundred years, however, nearly 80% of us in developing countries are now living to 65, and if you reach 65, you can expect another 16 years for men and 19 for women on the average. This extended longevity created a new developmental stage in the human life cycle, with enormous opportunities for psychological and spiritual growth. I share aging's revolutionary possibilities to remind you that we are not obsolete – our resilience fosters a creative and resourceful maturity.

Rabbi Schachter-Shalomi, the founder of Saging International, explains that "Elderhood represents the crowning achievement of life" and Jean Houston adds, "The years beyond sixty, the years of our second maturity, may be evolution's greatest gift to humanity." Carl Jung, that famous psychoanalyst, says that old age would not exist unless it had an evolutionary purpose, and spiritual author Angeles Arrien confirms, "The second half of life is the ultimate initiation. In it, we encounter those new, unexpected, unfamiliar, and unknowable moments that remind us that we are a sacred mystery made manifest. If we truly understand what is required of us at this stage, we are blessed with an enormous opportunity to develop and embody wisdom and character."

In sum, aging is a disguise that hides a profound process of psychological growth and spiritual evolution. This growth is not trivial, rather it creates the fertile ground, a new stage of life. I characterize its dynamics as the *Three Secrets of Aging*.

Secret I. Aging is an Initiation into an Extraordinary New Stage of Life. The key word here is Initiation. The secret tells us that the events and processes of aging – changing bodies, fading identities, and losses of all shapes and sizes – represent an initiation into an entirely new stage of life, a time of personal and spiritual growth unprecedented in human history. While aging may represent the end of our old life, it is also the beginning of a new one.

To understand this secret, we need to look at the nature of initiation. In its simplest form, initiation means being moved from one state or stage of life to another. Indigenous cultures understood this better than we do and created rituals to place it in a sacred context as rites of passage. Because modern retirement and birthday parties usually fail as real initiations, life itself initiates us through the natural shocks of aging, like the ending of your work life, declining health and physical vitality, the death of a friend or spouse, or a world catastrophe like the one confronting us now. But the point is this: whatever changes your life, whatever ends your old life and pushes you into a new one, is your initiation. It can be medical, economic, social or emotional; it can be a big event like this global crisis or an accumulation of little ones that push you over the tipping point – but you know without a doubt that your life has been forever changed. Suddenly huge questions rise up inside: "Who am I now?" "What do I do with myself?" "What is this time for?" "What is my role in the world's problems?" and "How will I face my future, including debility and death?" These questions initiate a vision quest for a new self and new life. It's time to grow again!

Secret II. Aging Is a Transformation of Self and Consciousness. Secret II says that "you" and the identity you've had your whole life disappears in aging, potentially opening space for a new and wiser you. How can that happen?

To begin with, I think it's pretty obvious that much of the "you" you used to be is disappearing or long gone. Is your body the same as it was in the middle years? How about your appearance? Do you still play the same social roles – parent, worker, householder – or have the same identity that you had during the career and family years? Instead of all that, now you wear this funny disguise of an aged person. Look in the mirror: there is almost nothing left of the old you! If that's not transformation, I don't know what is! But all this is only the beginning.

This disappearance of the old self – body, appearance, career, and identity – is part of the emptying of aging. It's like tacking a jigsaw puzzle picture of your life on the wall and then watching the pieces begin to fall off. What's the alternative to the continuing charade of the old you? The first answer involves the continuing evolution of the true self – who we really are inside, who we were born to be, our most natural self. It blossoms anew like a flower, especially as performance pressures from the persona fade away. Individuation does not stop in aging, it continues. And this is wonderful – new interests, emerging talents, creative self-expression – all sorts of things emerge from the revitalized psyche. This is the psychological dimension of Secret II – the authentic self, finally free from the responsibilities and goals of the middle years, grows anew, its gifts and talents often surprising us. And relevant to the theme of resilience, we will discover an expanding capacity to deal with the world's mounting challenges.

A second path through Secret II takes us into the spiritual dimension. Since most of what we used to be is now just thought and memory, what would happen if we momentarily stopped thinking and reciting the story of "me" and examined what is left? What is it that remains when thinking ceases? The answer is consciousness. It's always here, and if we focus increasingly on consciousness, something shifts. We no longer believe and identify so much with our thoughts. They are just thoughts. We are not what we think! We are the consciousness in which thought arises.

With this realization, aging becomes profoundly spiritual. We discover that consciousness is not just in me, I am in it, and it is everywhere. Ageless, timeless, eternal, and pure, transformative – this is consciousness. Then, if we're particularly perceptive, we may realize that this consciousness is sacred. Becoming conscious of consciousness itself, therefore, can evoke the experience of the divine Presence both inside and around you. Take a moment to reflect on this amazing possibility. Gifts of understanding, wisdom and courage can flow directly from the divine Self within. This discovery is like Galileo proclaiming that the sun, not the Earth, is the center of the universe. Now the ego is no longer the center of the personality, divine consciousness is. We will learn much more about this possibility in Part III.

Secret III. Aging is a Revelation of the Sacred Earth. As the distracting problems and goals of our old identity dissolve in conscious aging, we find ourselves drawn back into Creation. We get out of our heads and into our senses, and discover that the Earth is incredibly beautiful, amazing, and precious. We see again with new eyes and the innocence of childhood. We come home from our long journey through the world of identity, time and story to celebrate a radically new consciousness of the world around us.

This secret may be viewed from psychological or spiritual perspectives. The psychological dimension announces the growth of a new life following the reawakening of our true self: new interests, friends, and creative expression even in the midst of difficult times. This secret also involves a spiritual awakening. As self-preoccupation dissolves, we shift from *conceiving* the natural environment through the lens of social and scientific beliefs, to *perceiving* it in thought-free sensory wonder. In quiet moments in the garden, we sense that the sacredness of Creation is still here, we've just been ignoring it. In the shift, our love for the natural world grows, stirring a heartfelt motivation to heal the world. As we will see, this perceptual restoration is critical to the Earth's healing.

Conclusions

This first chapter was written to remind all of us older folk that psychological development continues in aging, unveiling a new stage of growth, a revitalized self, and profound appreciation of the sacred Earth. We are more creative, pliable, loving and perceptive. And, as we will see, profound new gifts germinate in this fertile soil. Although the historical times are dark, we are neither broken nor bereft, indeed whether our rapidly changing reality is devastating or creative, a dark night or new birth, a curse or a blessing, may be up to us. With years of experience under our belts, the wisdom of age, and the ongoing growth of psyche and soul, we will find vision, hope and courage for the road ahead.

Recommendations

1. This is a new stage of life so try to let go of old beliefs and assumptions. Clean your slate for unexpected realizations, goals and possibilities to emerge. It's all new.
2. Can you identify with the events and processes described here? Your self wants to grow anew and the Earth invites you back into Creation. These themes will recur throughout the book. For now, plant them like seeds in your imagination.
3. Realizing that the Earth, rediscovered in thought-free consciousness, is Creation, spend time outside. Awakened perception holds the key to the Earth's healing.

Chapter 2

More Good News: We Come with New Maturity

The Three Secrets of Aging prepares the psyche for new growth. In this chapter, we work its fertile ground to cultivate the emerging gifts of our new maturity. We don't get wise just by being old, there is work to do, and dark times need not undermine that work. In fact, work during hard times will focus it on the hard times! This chapter explores the maturational tasks of aging and the fruits we gather and share in this new season of life. Let's do some work.

The Tasks of Aging

Listed below are the major tasks of aging, tasks that turn aging into gifts of wisdom and maturity. To do this work, read the list as a whole, check the items that stir something inside, and then reflect on the insights or feelings that came to mind. Ask yourself how you feel and what work still needs to be done. Consider each item as a personal question to ponder and a universal conundrum to inspire growth. Then go a little deeper into these tasks in any way you like – journal writing, contemplation, therapy, spiritual direction, or conversations with friends. The purpose of this exercise is to understand how much you have already grown and identify any additional work you need to do. Don't rush through this exercise. Go deep!

The Tasks of Aging

Releasing the Identity and Roles of the Middle Years
Discovering the Language and Wisdom of the Aging Body
Learning to Grieve and Survive
Finding the Hidden Meaning and Value of Change

Life Review and Understanding
Growing the Unfinished Self
Finding Meaningful "Work"
Clarifying Religious and Spiritual Beliefs
Opening the Heart
Staying Involved
Facing the Personal Reality of Death

The Gifts of Aging

The psychological and spiritual self we nurture in conscious aging yields many gifts. Whatever your story, I am certain that aging's work in your life has already been fruitful. Still, it's important to recognize, describe and cultivate these gifts, for ignored, they may pass unnoticed and unrealized. We begin with the gifts we receive by working the Tasks of Aging. Once again, go deeply into these items to fully appreciate and understand them.

Gifts We Receive

Confidence in the Ability to Survive Tragedy, Hardship and Loss
Greater Patience, Maturity and Wisdom
Less Concern about What Others Think
Freedom from Traditional Social Roles and Expectations
New or Revived Interests and Hobbies
Healing and Reorganization of Personality
Psychological and Spiritual Insights about the Meaning of Life
A Deeper Experience of Community
An Easier and Less Conflicted Death

This next list consists of gifts we now have to give that ripened naturally through the seasons of life. Imagine how each might be shared or expressed. Describe your reflections and feelings. What are you learning?

Gifts We Have to Give

Encouragement, Support, and Reassurance
Practical Experience and Ideas
Blessing
Larger Vision of Life
A Personal Understanding of History
Stability
Social Conscience
Unconditional Love
The Ripened Self
Examples of How to Age and Die

Conclusions

We often forget or dismiss how much we have learned and grown in our lives, and, as a consequence, overlook or minimize our gifts. But our gifts grow into powerful resources for coping, caring, understanding and engaging. Reflect on your life and consider these developing capacities. We are calmer, stronger, tougher and wiser. We are more confident, patient and flexible in dealing with problems. Our personalities are better integrated and our insights richer. We value community more deeply and know its importance in coping with problems big and small. We have survived previous hardships and losses and know we can again. We have grown spiritually and reflected thoughtfully on our own death. As a result of this new wisdom and maturity, our support and encouragement mean so much more to each other and to younger generations, not only through our practical knowledge but through our deeper understanding of life, history, and spirituality. The love from our ripened self is more patient, unconditional, conscious and mature, and the appreciation we give others is sacred. Even our courage in facing death is a gift to those who one day will be in our shoes.

I hope you can now see how valuable you have become in age. Not perfect – who is? – but good enough. Can you remember a time when an older person gave you something special just by paying attention to you, caring about your problems, or sharing practical knowledge? I know it's easy to feel useless and unimportant at times, but you are anything but, for age has blessed you and now you can bless others. Look around. Who might you call, visit, help or invite into your life? These acts are not inconsequential or meaningless, they are sacred gifts that blossomed from your Tree of Life. Share them.

Recommendations

1. Review these tasks and gifts often as medicine for feelings of uselessness and doubt.
2. Keep expanding your understanding of these tasks and gifts, unlocking more ideas, opportunities, and possibilities.
3. Gifts are empty if not received or given. Try out these gifts. Feel good about the ones you received and share the ones you have to give. Then watch your confidence and power grow.

Chapter 3

Bad News: The Approaching Storm Is Huge

Now we come to the hard part. I believe that telling the truth about the global crisis is critical to our preparation as older people. Attempts to minimize or sugar-coat reality make the world more dangerous not less, and they insult our intelligence. Our generation can handle the truth. Hardship is real. The danger is real. We do not need to be protected from scientific facts or bad news. I am not afraid to call this time an apocalypse.

I know this material is hard to face but I cannot apologize for being an alarmist – the global alarms have been sounding for years and now they are screaming. We've long known about infectious diseases, global warming, unrestrained population growth, and the breakdown of civilization as we know it. The fate of our species now hangs in the balance. If we are going to confront this worldwide crisis as a human family, we have to face it. The Earth is crying out for our help in the loudest way she knows how – by threatening our very existence. Here is a concise summary of the world's existential threats though they will change as events play out. Digest the facts but hold your feelings for now – a chance to express them is coming.

The Novel Coronavirus (COVID-19)

The novel coronavirus was first reported in China in late December, 2019. The virus probably jumped from Pangolins butchered in "wet markets" to humans in a process called zoonotic transmission. It is only one of several similar infectious viral diseases, including MERS and SARS. Bacterial zoonotic infectious diseases also threaten the world with illnesses like anthrax, bird flu, Lyme disease, Ebola, and the Bubonic plague but are more effectively treated with antibiotics. Epidemiologists expect that 70% of the world will eventually be exposed to the coronavirus with older people disproportionally endangered (mortality rates currently estimated at 8% between 70 and 79 and 15% over 80). As the numbers of infections and deaths grew around the world, we learned how unprepared most countries, governments and hospitals were for handling such an epidemic and scenes of immense suffering ensued. We also learned that the virus could also cycle back through the population, possibly in seasonal waves, eventually settling in permanently unless scientists develop a successful vaccine. While the majority of the infected will survive, many with absent or minor symptoms, may experience more serious consequences including pneumonia and the catastrophic buildup of pulmonary fluid leading to death (Acute Respiratory Distress Syndrome). There is much we don't know about this virus. To mitigate against this highly contagious and expanding public health threat, numerous states and countries moved to close borders and shutter schools, restaurants, entertainment venues, and businesses, in addition to prescribing temporary self-quarantines or even total population lockdowns. The World Health Organization declared the coronavirus a global pandemic.

The Climate Crisis

The Earth is getting hotter every year. Heat-trapping CO_2 is higher than it's been in 3 million years and the last five years have been the hottest on record. It's called the "Greenhouse Effect." Why is this important? Rising heat radically supercharges the weather all over the Earth, creating dangerous heat spells; ferocious hurricanes, tornados and forest fires; monsoon rains; expanding deserts; dying oceans; coastal flooding; inland draughts; an escalating tide of climate refugees; and massive species extinction. Climate scientists say we are facing a possible collapse of biological and social systems threatening civilization as we know it. In fact, a consortium of 11,000 scientists from

153 nations made this announcement November, 2019, "We declare clearly and unequivocally that planet Earth is facing a climate emergency,... The climate crisis has arrived and is accelerating faster than most scientists expected. It is more severe than anticipated, threatening natural ecosystems and the fate of humanity." And the lead negotiator for the Paris climate agreement added in February, "What's at stake over the next decade is nothing less than the future of the planet and of humanity on the planet. That's no exaggeration, that is no hyperbole. That is actually scientific fact."

The Population Explosion

Adding to this expanding nightmare is the mounting pressure of population explosion. When America was founded, there were less than one billion people on Earth. When I was a child in the fifties, the world had 2.6 billion people. Now it's 7.7 billion. By 2050, we will exceed 9 billion people on Earth. Because we lack the sustainable resources to feed this growing population, we borrow dangerously from the future – draining aquifers, cutting down forests for farming, over-fishing the oceans, and poisoning ourselves and nature with pesticides and plastics. Earth's growing overpopulation will result in polluted water and air; superbugs and new parasites, microplastics in our oceans, soil, air, snow, and bodies; overwhelmed hospitals; rising crime; more deforestation and wildlife deaths; widespread food shortages; regional conflicts over food and clean water; desperate migrations, and even war.

The Breakdown of Civilization

In the wake of the desperate social-distancing measures to contain the coronavirus, unemployment skyrocketed, consumers reduced spending, stock markets roiled, and the economy headed into recession, creating financial hardship and insecurities throughout the world. While a restoration of normalcy may begin to occur as the epidemic comes under control, it will be quickly tested by the rapidly worsening climate crisis, for global warming affects the stability of civilization itself. Excessively high temperatures disrupt agriculture, harm health, and shut down energy webs; extreme weather threatens water and transportation; loss of property in storm disasters can bankrupt insurance companies; and coastal flooding will overwhelm vulnerable oil refineries like those on the Gulf Coast and Northern California. Social and political instability, climate-caused infrastructure damage, and the challenge of retooling the military to non-fossil fuels also pose severe national and global security threats. Traditional capitalism itself is now literally unsustainable because it relies so heavily on continuing economic and population growth in a system of finite and overtaxed resources. Last but not least, the inaction and political agenda of elected officials represents a horrifying obstacle to timely action. After Brazil's president gave the green light to illegal land invasion, deforestation in the Brazilian Amazon surged past three football fields a minute; and the U.S. president steadily deregulates environmental protections and threatens to withdraw from the Paris Climate Agreement. Because of our global interdependence, these systemic risks represent collective vulnerabilities to the fabric of civilization as we know it. No one and no place is immune.

As implied above, these four disasters all interact, extending and potentiating each other's harmful effects. For example, global warming can enable the further spread of infectious diseases by increasing areas of optimum temperatures and humidity, accelerate flood-induced water-borne illnesses, release ancient viruses and bacteria from land exposed by melting glaciers, and spread diseases via insects and rodents migrating to warmer climes. Similarly, farming or business practices that invade, alter or reduce wild ecosystems, sequester animals in crammed pens, increase human-animal contact, capture exotic animals and sell wild animals as pets, all increase the risks of animal to human transmission. As the social architecture of emergency workers, military and police forces, agricultural and transportation systems, hospital and medical facilities, and electrical and water infrastructures frays, so too will the social safety net and civilized behavior.

Conclusions

The Earth is crying out for our help. This "Crisis in Creation" affects every living being, and everyone has a part to play addressing it. No one individual can "save the world," but all of us doing what we can do – mitigating personal consumption and waste, applying personal expertise to local problems, and taking political action – combined with large scale government programs and international cooperation, may slowly turn the tide of global warming or at least arrest its worst outcomes. Nonetheless, we will soon face ever more difficult conditions and it's time for the older generation – you and me – to prepare and mobilize. Specifically, we need to improve our psychological and spiritual coping strategies, bring our gifts to the world-wide effort, and reflect on the ultimate meaning and purpose of this time. We have more work ahead.

Recommendations

1. Honor yourself for honestly facing these hard facts.
2. Learn how dysfunctional human behavior and environmentally-destructive systems are harming your own area and what you can do to help.
3. Get in touch with the feelings evoked by these facts. Not only must they be managed, they can source the energy and motivation necessary for constructive action.

Part II. Guidance for Emotional Survival

The bad news just reviewed is terrifying. You may be tempted to bolt the door, hide under the bed, and give up. I completely understand. While collecting climate data over the past couple of years, I tried to convince myself countless times everything will work out, that answers would come, that the threat was exaggerated. But it's not going that way and hiding won't save us. But lest we forget, we are in a creative new stage of life characterized by hard-won resilience, a resource-filled self, and an awakening love for Creation. Let's build on that. Part II provides guidance for coping with overwhelming emotions, applying psychological and spiritual understanding to personal growth and resilience, and transforming terrible distress into soulful action. It's a blueprint for emotional survival, spiritual growth, and personal transformation.

Chapter 4

Coping with Overwhelming Emotions: It's Possible!

Here is my personal confession and it's true: For several months in 2019, I felt haunted. I would wake up at 5:00 am with skin-crawling dread because everywhere I went, I could see ten years into the future, daily witnessing the new "Four Horsemen" of our global apocalypse riding roughshod over the planet. Perhaps these visions were a product of a fevered imagination. Perhaps they are only partly true. Perhaps the horror is coming. Have you experienced such dread-inspiring visions? I don't share them to frighten you, only to give voice to my own fears, acknowledge yours, and mobilize both of us to care more and more for the world. Here's what I saw.

I saw hillsides of dead trees in the Pacific Northwest riddled with beetles, tinder for coming infernos; I saw dry stream beds, like parched cracked throats, spreading through the Sierra Nevada and Cascade Mountains of Western America; I saw fish, faunae and two-leggeds dying across the globe because glaciers no longer fill their life-giving rivers; I saw 150 species of plants and animals going extinct every day – it's called the Sixth Extinction, with our beloved salmon and whale populations disappearing in warming, polluted, acidic oceans and streams; I saw exhausted immigrant families fleeing the over-population, suffocating heat, useless fields, and failing economies of their homelands only to be cruelly driven back by soldiers; I saw once great cities replaced by deserted dusty wastelands, and whole towns and villages turned into graveyards by rampaging parasites, superbugs, and the starvation of failed crops; I saw the old and sick struggling with neither medications nor hospitals; I saw agitated parents searching depleted grocery shelves to fill near-empty pantries and dead refrigerators; I saw skies swallowed by rotating jet-black storm systems, vast and demonic, two hundred-mile-per-hour winds and crushing rains, churning toward incredulous, hypnotized onlookers frozen in fear; and I saw the rise of authoritarian governments, failed states, civil wars, and the domino-like collapse of lawful civilization as peoples and nations fight for power and resources. I was living in two alternating realities unable to share my insane double-vision with anyone. Sometimes I found myself crying, and all the while, I heard the dark threatening bass riff from Jaws playing in my head. I thought, "That can't be good."

Many people still cannot see these dangers, and I can't stop seeing them – heartbreaking and terrifying. I join climate scientists trembling in fear from their own findings and doctors struggling in overwhelmed hospitals with insufficient equipment, meds and beds. My escalating anxiety insists that I wake up and pay attention: I am feeling the suffering of Creation Herself. How about you?

We are Creation and we will suffer as she grows sicker. There is no place to hide and nowhere else to go. Nor will inept politicians and oil-corrupted lobbyists save us. We need to take a massive stand for life now or follow this haunting vision to its prophesied ending. The scientific debate over the threat of pandemics, climate change, population growth and civilization breakdown has ended. So, too, must denial, ignorance, passivity and cynicism yield to empirical facts and internationally-coordinated action. But what can we do with our rapidly mounting fear and despair? Our work must begin with ourselves.

Responding to Crises in Four Dimensions

As a psychologist, minister, and writer on conscious aging, I see this impending crisis in four dimensions: practical, psychological, spiritual, and the wisdom of the sage. Let's spend some time in each dimension and see how it might add to our coping resources.

The Practical Dimension. Obviously, we need to survive. We need the basics – water, food, shelter, medicine, safety. We also need an accurate account of what's happening in the world from week to week to act accordingly. The more we plan in advance for long-term adaptation, the better our chances of survival. Science, technology, and government action are critical and many strategies are already being implemented as the global drama builds. Most importantly, we need to create functioning and sustainable local systems for providing basic needs. Community building can also provide emotional support, creative problem-solving, and hope. This first dimension exceeds the scope of this book but all of us – from individuals to local, state and national governments – need to keep focusing on practical and community adaptation.

The Psychological Dimension. When we lift the lid of denial, the magnitude of our impending trauma feels crushing and unbearable. Its scale is terrifying and mounting grief can break our resolve and our spirits. We erupt angrily, hide in denial, or go numb, responses consistent with our deepest animal instincts of fight, flight, or freeze. Tragically, a fourth emotional response also beckons – collapsing in despair as hope dwindles. None of these reactions will help us adapt to this changing world. We need to manage our distress instead. Here are some ideas for coping with overwhelming emotions. Explore them slowly, there is a lot to digest here.

What we need most in the beginning is mutual support, compassion and understanding, tenderly holding our shattered and frightened hearts until basic stability returns and healing can begin. Loss hurts so much. With each setback, death, or disorienting shock, we are, for a time, too broken and traumatized to act constructively. We must give our pain time, understanding and acceptance to move through us. Don't be impatient with your feelings, instead make space to emote them one painful catharsis at a time. Keep in mind, too, that coping with the grief of traumatic loss continues for years. The death of a loved one is never really healed, but it can be managed, shared, honored, and made sacred. Dealing with loss is the work of unfinished love and the work of a lifetime.

Feelings are not reality but they need to be processed to prevent paralysis and resume effective action. But remember that anything we feel changes as we feel it. That's what "working through" means. Painful emotions gradually release their raw immediate energy and pass, permitting us to regain a degree of control, see our situation more clearly again, and respond proactively. Though grief goes with us forever, we can recover purpose and action, fight on to save other loved ones, and work to rebuild civilization. On the other hand, working through does not mean "acting out." While anger and blame directed at each other can discharge emotion, it is counterproductive, causing recurring cycles of pain and reactivity on all fronts.

We also need to feel our feelings to recover who we are. When we bury feelings too long, we lose our self, we grow numb and inert, we start dying emotionally. Akin to burnout and battle fatigue, too much unprocessed pain takes us down. It's usually easy enough to see, but not so easy to heal. Catch it early. Create "therapy" sessions for each other every day. Provide loving feedback. Recovering means feeling again no matter how awful the feelings. When help doesn't work, take time out if possible and get out of the battle. Rest and safety are medicine, too.

The constant pain of unbearable circumstances must also be managed, and there is a way. From his horrific World War II concentration camp experience, psychologist Victor Frankl found that we find meaning, purpose and love by focusing on the each other's needs in the present moment. When we take care of each other in the timeless now, we get out of our heads and awaken the power of love. One day at a time, one gesture, kind word or helping hand, knits the fabric in love that makes life bearable. A touch, a story, a memory, a joke, a poem, an observation – we each have something to give. As Mr. Rogers' mother counseled, in times of crisis, "look for the helpers." Even now, even as things unravel around us, there are so many people trying to do the right thing.

Working through feelings also offers new insights into ourselves and others. What do your emotional reactions say about your values, assumptions and beliefs, and what else may be going on inside you that is important but not obvious? Sometimes new wounds expose old ones and we get paralyzed in the unfinished business of life. Other times, new insights catalyze new ways of thinking that move us from reactivity to psychological understanding, clearer focus, and better planning. All problem-solving has an emotional level that, unrecognized, can impede progress, but managed will produce more energy, creativity and commitment for change.

Always remember community. Rather than isolating ourselves in fortresses of fear and paranoia for survival, we need to stay in community. Remember that isolation breeds depression, hopelessness, and fear; especially in sustained crises, community is the cure. Divided, we cower, together we can be an amazing force of healing, creativity and commitment. Reach out. Share meals. Play games. Be there for each other.

Finally, continually assess reality. What's happening right now? How are things changing? Which problems are receding and which growing? Reality is evolving, too. When time for action comes, it needs to be grounded in an objective awareness of actual circumstances.

The Spiritual Dimension. Everyone has personal spiritual beliefs of one sort or another – beliefs about ultimate issues like the meaning of life, the value of love, the nature of suffering, what happens at death, and the transcendent dimension by whatever name. These beliefs may be religious, humanistic, aesthetic, cosmological, or grounded in scientific wonder and awe. And we have all had experiences that evoked spiritual questions and intuitions. One of the gifts of spirituality is that it can provide a supportive framework of hope and coping in times of hardship or crisis.

When terrible things happen, we ask profound questions about the significance of the event that go beyond physical facts to the level of transcendent meaning and causation. Our spiritual and religious beliefs, readings, and prayers can stir answers and comfort us, help us bear the unbearable, find new meaning of our struggle, and provide hope for the future. They can also deepen our connection with the divine through prayer, contemplation, meditation, ritual, fasting, art and dance. By creating a real and felt connection to the sacred, we experience religious truths for ourselves and kindle new depths of love and compassion.

With these goals and values in mind, here are some recommendations for working in the spiritual dimension. Ask yourself the big spiritual questions like, "Where is God in this crisis?" "What are my spiritual beliefs about what's happening?" "What is my spiritual purpose or work here?" and "What might the world's crisis suggest about humanity's spiritual evolution?" Your intuitive answers can reframe hardships as meaningful. Ponder what the world's great spiritual teachers might tell you about your situation and how to respond. Read your favorite spiritual texts and look for their inspiration and guidance. Return to your spiritual practices, like prayer, meditation, or yoga. They can restore emotional stability and renew spiritual values. Let your beliefs and practices awaken the love, compassion and courage inherent in their teachings, and realize that facing painful realities is itself a spiritual practice.

Finally, considerable psychological research in recent years has validated the role of religion and spirituality in supporting community, reducing drug and alcohol abuse and addiction, reducing delinquency and criminal behavior, promoting positive health habits, and coping with loss, divorce, and mental health challenges including suicide. When spirituality is tied to religious commitment and attendance, community becomes an even more powerful source for buffering stress and protecting members.

The Wisdom of the Sage. As we grow older, we integrate our life experience, practical survival skills, evolving self, and psychological and spiritual resources to nourish the wisdom of the sage – one who can stand in the fire, stay focused, and provide meaningful and inspiring leadership. We find the authority of the moral voice, a voice that speaks for humanity, all sentient beings, and future generations. Here are ideas for working with the emerging wisdom of the sage in your own life.

Use the practical savvy acquired in sixty, seventy, eighty or more years of life to approach problems from a wiser perspective. This is not your first rodeo. You've survived hard times before. Remember how you did it. Review the most important lessons learned in your life. Use them to create your most mature and loving self, a self who can act bravely and constructively in a chaotic world. Find your own voice and speak clearly, calmly, consciously. Speak with the wisdom of your ancestors and the rights of future generations in mind. Stand behind your words. Build loving community with all people – friends, strangers, adversaries alike – as well as beings from the animal and plant kingdoms. Use non-adversarial communication and deep listening. Don't talk at or over people, listen with your heart and ask deep and sincere questions. Invite everyone to participate in creating solutions. And finally, learn to live in the sacred consciousness of Secret II to act in ways untethered from fear, reactivity and self-centered motivations.

The Alchemical Power of Emotion

Alchemy was the medieval father of chemistry, a philosophy and methodology that attempted to transmute base metal into gold and find an elixir for curing disease and prolonging life. Looking back, psychologists realized that its theories symbolically described the profound transformation of the psyche, as when one feeling state completely turns into another. It is a powerful and dramatic description of emotional healing.

As a clinical psychologist, I learned that any traumatic emotions that we are willing to experience directly, to bear deeply and honestly, will change, and will change us, expanding our coping capacity, compassion and our love. As a spiritual person, I learned that whatever distress we feel about the Earth is the Earth speaking through us, because we are the Earth. We are part of Creation and she will guide us. We must understand, then, that the feelings and emotions triggered by this Earth crisis, however difficult, have the potential to evolve and transform us. In other words, feelings and beliefs, experienced in the transformational fires of sacred consciousness, eventually transmute into higher forms, like coal into diamond, base metal into gold, or humanity into divinity, for consciousness finds the sacred in everything because consciousness is itself sacred.

For example, it's my fervent belief that...

Creation Anxiety, our intense and soul-shattering fear for the Earth and her beings, experienced directly in awakened consciousness, can ignite transformational fires inside that will one day bring fearless action. In divinity's spiritual furnace, we are recast into new beings.

It's my fervent belief that...

Creation Despair, experienced in genuine, full-throated, heart-breaking grief about the dying world, will one day unleash the power to act for the Earth without compromise or mortal concern. We get up one morning, know what we have to do, and we start doing it.

And it's my fervent belief that...

Creation Rage, our fury at what petroleum products, toxic chemicals, Earth-raping development, endless waste, self-dealing politicians, collective ignorance and everyday carelessness are still doing to our Mother, can be transformed through education, restraint, integrity, enlightened vision, scientific guidance, and political action, so that one day, in the not-too-awfully-distant future, we will see our pain and anger transmuted into a new and sustainable way of life on Earth.

In sum, directly experiencing our Creation-related distress in pure, intense and awakened consciousness can prepare us to act for Creation with courage, sacrifice and determination. Feel it, be patient, go deep, and action will come. And act we must.

Conclusions

Given what we are up against in this global crisis, it is not surprising that we often feel overwhelmed and helpless, but we can manage overwhelming emotions by working our distress in practical, psychological and spiritual ways, all the while tapping into the creative resources cultivated in mature aging. In this alchemical process, we realize the wisdom of sage and the power of transformation. Yes, we still lapse back into old patterns of reactivity from time to time, but we sense the way forward, pick up the pieces, and step into the fray again. To further support this process, more advice on coping and helping is coming in the next chapter.

Recommendations

1. We sometimes feel too overwhelmed to act constructively. Continually processing our distress in the four dimensions will channel its inchoate energies and bring new tools to the problem. In fact, doing anything constructive will help because focused action stabilizes the psyche.

2. Be sure to spend time in each dimension. Focusing on only one or two will limit your possibilities and your sense of control. More doing, more control, more growth.

3. Whatever you do, hold yourself, your family, your community, and Creation in love. Practice love all the time. Ask yourself, "What would love do here?" Love is the one deep and abiding resource that never runs out as long as we work through the pain and reactivity that sometimes cause us to forget.

Chapter 5

Preparing for Battle: A Practical Workbook for Resilience

We now move from theory to practice. Our goal is to transform understanding into personal growth, increased resilience and greater stability to prepare ourselves for the coming storm. Chapter 5 presents checklists for coping with overwhelming emotions, managing depression, cultivating personal growth and instilling hope, followed by exercises for reducing anxiety and restoring life-promoting feelings of gratitude. It's a practical workbook for increasing our resilience in difficult times. You'll notice that some list items repeat across topics because they are more universal. Finally, don't rush through this material. Follow the instructions and carefully engage each checklist and exercise – you are working on your life.

Checklists

Coping with Overwhelming Emotions. Here are things you can do to manage overwhelming emotions. Make a check mark beside the behaviors you already do and circle others that might be good for you.

- Exercise – it always helps with stress
- Express your feelings – talk with friends, find or start a support group, get a therapist, write in your journal, cry, be mad, be sad, don't bottle up emotions
- Meditate – quiet those frightened obsessive thoughts
- Use spiritual practices – consider yoga, tai chi, contemplation, positive affirmations and prayer to stay calm and centered
- Educate yourself and others – new information brings

new ideas, resources, and coping strategies

- Join activist organizations – like the Environmental Defense Fund, Sunrise Movement, Extinction Rebellion, Sierra Club, Elders Action Network, or Creation Spirituality Communities and become politically active
- Do normal things that feel normal – like reading, playing with pets, cleaning house or gardening, it returns a bit of sanity to everyday life
- Play – board games, puzzles and online cat videos to raise your mood
- Listen to music – sing out loud, dance in your living room, soothing or rock, is good for the soul
- Stop and breathe – use breath as a moment of peace and clarity
- Get enough sleep
- Spend time with loved ones – online or in-house, love your homies
- Connect everyday with nature – walks, gardening, animal watching reconnects you with Creation and she will inspire you with her amazing diversity and creativity

Looking back over your checks and circles, what do you notice? What activities have been most helpful? What else might you do? Write three positive resolutions for change. Repeat this checklist whenever you feel lost in emotion.

Managing Depression. Dos and Don'ts. In graduate school, we conducted research on depression from a behavioral perspective. We developed a list of "pleasant events," that is, activities people enjoyed or found positively reinforcing, and used a brief psychological inventory to track depressive symptoms. Each day our depressed clients recorded the number of pleasant activities they did and rated the severity of their down mood. Invariably we found that these two variables were inversely related: more pleasant activities, less depression, and less pleasant activities, more depression. Drawing on this principle and related research, here is a list of dos and don'ts for combatting depression. Check the items most important to you.

Do...

- Make a list of pleasant events – things you like to do and do one or more every day
- Talk regularly about feelings with family, friends, neighbors, or caregivers – it will relieve depression and deepen community
- Know when you need professional help and get it – at some point in life, we all need therapy, it's no different than going to the doctor for other problems
- Practice "thought-stopping" when you're stuck in a negative mental loop – stand still, get focused, and give yourself the command, "Stop," remain without thought for 5 seconds, then get involved with something practical
- Get a pet – they provide company, love, and playful entertainment
- Make friends with an indoor plant – research shows that tender and attentive care of a plant actually improves our mood and returns a sense of purpose to daily life.
- Participate in a church, synagogue or mosque – spirituality and community can relieve loneliness and return meaning to life
- Maintain a healthy lifestyle – eat balanced meals, get enough sleep, exercise regularly, reduce smoking, alcohol, caffeine and binge eating.
- Take classes online – stimulate your intellect
- Join educational, climate activist or 12-step support groups – stay involved in life
- Find a fun or interesting new hobby – you might be surprised by how it ends up helping the world

- Read inspirational books – keep looking for enlightening ideas
- Practice empathy and love for others – you will feel useful and love ends up going both ways
- Stay busy – activity channels stress and gets things done
- Maintain a positive attitude – look for the upside of events, personal efforts, and daily life
- Be flexible – if one thing doesn't work, try another
- Add more items that apply to you – be your own coach

Don't...

- Isolate yourself psychologically – it reinforces feelings of loneliness and despair
- Dwell constantly on negative thoughts and feelings – they will take you further down
- Medicate feelings with alcohol or drugs – short-term numbness costs long-term problems
- Lose yourself in self-isolating video games – aloneness brings depression
- Believe strange conspiracy theories or join hateful organizations – you have enough challenges without invented ones
- Take out your feelings on those around you – it generates more hurt
- Give up hope – it is the heartbeat of life
- Add more items and don't do them
- Be critical of yourself – you don't have to be perfect, good enough is good enough

Review your checked items. Think about how to increase the dos and decrease the don'ts. Make a start and keep track of your success.

Cultivating Personal Growth. This is not the time to let curiosity or personal growth stagnate. Here is a list of activities that will bring you back to life, strengthen your adjustive resources, and help build a better world (even while sheltering in place).

- Re-imagine your life as a story overcoming hardship, then begin doing it – it might actually start happening
- Learn something new – what have you always wanted to understand and why?
- Explore creative new ways to adapt, thrive and solve problems – take a current problem and brainstorm three new approaches to it (remember brainstorming means thinking without instant criticism)
- Imagine yourself as fully realized – picture what you would you be doing right now
- Challenge yourself to be the "best you" in a difficult situation – describe that self in action
- Pursue distance learning with online courses, visit virtual museums, try online travel to interesting places – choose one and describe what you found
- Make a list of things you always wanted to do and find one that fits your circumstances – do one and see what happens
- Read a self-help book on health, personal growth or spirituality – describe the advice you found most helpful and how you might use it in the future
- Write letters to people and tell them what they mean to you – old-fashioned letters are such a welcome surprise for everyone
- Write your memoirs – it generates personal growth leaves a legacy for future generations
- Reach out, help someone, or volunteer for a good cause – helping grows the soul
- Create art, music, poetry, dance or new meal recipes – creativity awakens the true self, pick one and see what happens

- Remember the best times in your life – recall who you were then and resurrect that person for now

Take one item and write about it. Discover its personal value and teaching. Work with another item. There is so much personal growth material here, you may be amazed by what you discover.

Instilling Hope through Good News. The negative news cycle diminishes hope, energy, and motivation. Every now and then, make your own list of good news. Consider news like...

- Lowered rates of coronavirus infection or death in the world
- Faster recovery from coronavirus infections
- Reports of successful vaccine trials or antiviral medications
- High tech solutions for removing plastics from our oceans, streams, land and air
- Evidence of politicians and countries mobilizing against global warming
- New scientific discoveries on arresting or coping with climate change
- Heart-warming reports of people helping one another, wildlife, or the Earth
- Indications of reduced levels of pollution in air, water and land
- Signs of environmental recovery
- Technological breakthroughs for energy production, clean air and water, sustainable farming, non-polluting packaging
- Evidence of successful population management
- Stories of improved conditions for women and children around the world
- Countries transcending war in favor of loving kindness
- Actions all can take to help Mother Earth back to health

- Keep adding topics and collecting good news
- Keep the lists. Share them with friends. Make a list of news you'd like to hear

Exercises

Reducing Anxiety. In frightening times, fear and anxiety can be immobilizing. Here is a multistep exercise for regaining control. Keep in mind that anxiety doesn't disappear instantly, we need to keep practicing these skills to retrain our psychological and physiological reactions.

1. *Preparation*. Find a time when you won't be interrupted or distracted and schedule a 20-minute relaxation session. Sit in a comfortable position and put aside any immediate worries. Consider this a brief time-out from stress. Before you begin, rate your anxiety from 1–10 (1 meaning no anxiety and 10 indicating near panic).

2. *Self-Massage*. Start by massaging tense muscles. Spend a minute massaging your forehead, face and scalp, then spend another minute on your neck and shoulders. If another part of your body feels particularly tense, work on it, too. Enjoy the massage; feel your muscles relaxing and appreciating the attention.

3. *Slow Your Breathing*. Focus now on your breath. Take a deep breath and let it out slowly. Do it again. Repeat this phrase and connect it to your breath: "Breath in to relax and out to let go." Now practice four-count breathing for a couple minutes: counting slowly from 1 to 4 for the inbreath and then 1–4 for the outbreath.

4. *Remember a Time of Deep Peace and Relaxation*. Vividly recall a time and place where you felt safe, relaxed, and deeply peaceful. It might have been on a vacation or during childhood. Take your time. Find a good one. When you have found such a memory, relive it in your imagination and be very specific. Where are you? What exactly do you

see around you? What do you hear? What sensations are you aware of? What do you smell in the environment? How do you feel in this memory? Begin to feel that again. Close your eyes and go even deeper into the memory. Enjoy it. When you're ready, open your eyes.

5. *Conclude with Positive Affirmations.* Reinforce your progress by repeating one or more of these positive affirmations until you feel its effects in your mind and body.

> *I am calm and relaxed.*
> *I feel more relaxed with every peaceful breath.*
> *I am capable of solving my problems.*
> *I know I can overcome anxiety.*
> *I replace negative thoughts with positive ones.*
> *Feelings of panic are leaving my body.*
> *My mind and body are calm.*

6. When you're ready, rate your level of anxiety again on the 1–10 scale, get up slowly, and move into your day. Continue the breath work and affirmations throughout the day as mini-practices to boost your progress.

As you explore this practice, note which parts are most powerful for you. Use them more or personalize this process in whatever way works. Like any other skill training, the key is to practice daily so keep at it. To assess your progress, chart your anxiety ratings.

Practicing Gratitude. Our experience of life is profoundly influenced by positive or negative attitudes. If we feel cheated, mistreated or bitter about the past, the future will be judged through the same negative filter and breed more unhappiness, loneliness and depression. An "attitude of gratitude" releases toxic emotional patterns, changes our brains' circuitry and hormones, and creates positive expectations that change our behavior. To start your gratitude practice, think of three adjectives that express your present mood and then write responses to these items in your journal.

1. Identify three things you feel grateful for
2. Identify three things you appreciate about yourself
3. Identify three people you appreciate in your life
4. Identify three things you feel grateful for about the Earth

Now find three more adjectives that describe your mood. What do you notice? From your experience, write a couple of positive mantras to repeat during the day to modify your reactions to the day's events.

Conclusions

This chapter has been a boot camp for emotional strength-training to boost resilience and personal coping. Psychologists call this ego-strength and it reflects our capacity to stand up under stress and maintain effective coping. Through checklists and practices, this chapter illustrates ways to increase our ego-strength, by learning ways to cope with overwhelming emotions and depression, cultivating personal growth and hope, and trading fear and anxiety for gratitude. Coping, cultivating, growing – these are some of the requisite skills for confronting the coming battles and helping the world. No one can repair the world alone but all of us just might be able to do it together. We are each part of the solution. Finding your part comes next.

Recommendations

1. Reinforce your overall personal growth by recording new insights and revelations in your journal. Ask yourself how they might renew vision, hope and courage.
2. Return to these checklists and exercises every time you feel stuck. Checklists are good ways to do checkups.
3. Become your own best friend, therapist, and coach. Stay positive and be sure to applaud your own progress.

Chapter 6

"How Can I Help?" Finding Your Gifts for the World

People frequently experience a desire to "give back" or "help the world" in times of crisis but are unsure what they have to offer, especially as they grow older. While the question, "How can I help?" may appear simple at first glance, "obvious" answers don't always lead to meaningful or committed engagement. For example, when I retired, I was surprised by how much resistance I felt to getting involved in the typical ways – volunteering at food banks, demonstrating for climate activism, joining environmental organizations. First of all, it felt like going back to work – I was done with the work grind and I didn't want a schedule or obligations. Second, the world's problems seemed so great, the obstacles so big, the answers so elusive, the possibilities so many, I just threw up my hands. Finally, there was the problem of finding something that really spoke to me personally, something both meaningful and motivating, and that proved to be more difficult than I imagined even though it was right under my nose! I now believe this personal challenge represents the most important element of all.

The question of how to "how to help" did not resolve for me until I finally accepted who I really was and what I really wanted to do. Why is this personal search so important and how do we do it? Theologian Howard Thurman offers an important clue. He said, "Don't ask yourself what the world needs. Ask yourself what makes you come alive, and go do that, because what the world needs is people who have come alive." My goal in this chapter is to help you answer Howard Thurman's question for yourself. What makes you come alive?

Discernment

In Chapter 2, we looked at the universal gifts uncovered through working the tasks of aging. Now it's time to look at your own personal gifts and unique calling through the process of discernment. From my professional experience, I view discernment from a spiritual and depth-oriented perspective implying a prolonged and heartfelt search for our true vocation. "Why am I really here?" and "What did I come here to do?" These kinds of questions begin to inspire a heartfelt journey into meaning and service.

For most of us, a calling or vocation need not involve some huge, lofty or grand enterprise, like ending cancer, war or world hunger. It's different than that. Listen to how Quaker author Parker Palmer puts it, "Vocation ... is something I can't not do, for reasons I'm unable to explain to anyone else and don't fully understand myself but that are nonetheless compelling." It's what you feel compelled by your very nature to do so that you can't not do it. Theologian Frederick Buechner adds this critically important ingredient, stating that vocation is "the place where your deep gladness meets the world's deep need." What is your deep gladness? And sacred activist Andrew Harvey wisely counsels, "follow your heartbreak," suggesting that whatever breaks open your heart is where you may be called to serve. Discernment is how we divine what these conundrums mean to us personally.

Discernment activities can be a particularly good focus for people over 65 searching for meaning and purpose in the later years. Indeed, the New Aging – this new developmental stage in the human life cycle – is perfectly suited to finding and expressing this uniquely personal work. From a spiritual perspective, I believe it's one of the reasons we're living so long in the first place. So, the key questions are, "Do you come alive in your work?" "Is it something you can't not do?" "Does it bring out your deep gladness?" And "Does it touch a place in your heart that's been opened by the world's pain?"

Finding the Gifts of Your Soul

Here is a visualization exercise to help you discern the work of your soul. You might record the instructions at timed intervals so you can close your eyes and participate fully. See what happens.

1. Close your eyes, and relax. (10 seconds)
2. Take a couple of deep breaths and settle comfortably into your chair, your body, your being. Take your time. Let this be a peaceful, gentle, and loving experience. (10 seconds)
3. Let your thoughts slow down and come to rest. Release the questions, distractions and issues of the day and center your attention deep inside, descending into the rich dark inner space of self or spirit. Breathe slowly and let each breath take you deeper. (10 seconds)
4. Now picture yourself standing by a clear pool of water in a beautiful natural setting on a lovely day. You might hear birds chirping or leaves rustling in the gentle breeze. Feel the warm sun on your face and shoulders. Smell the grass or dirt under your feet. Just be there, fully present, patient and trusting. (15 seconds)
5. You have come to this sacred pool to seek guidance in finding your own best way of "giving back." To help you succeed in this quest, silently call out for any friends, spirits, allies, ancestors, wisdom figures, angels or other beings whose support you value. Who do you want to support you in this inner search? Imagine asking them to come and help you understand and find this work of your soul. Picture them coming forward and standing around the water with you. Feel them joining you, aligning their highest energies with yours. (30 seconds)
6. Open also to the deep energies of the sacred Earth that hold and embrace you, to the stars and the cosmos that

sense your existence, and to the divine being, however you conceive it, and feel its loving Presence surround you. (30 seconds)

7. Now think of one question the discernment question stirs in you. Any question you like. Let that question become clear. Now, in the silence of this deep inner space, standing beside this pool, supported by wise and loving beings, silently ask that question and look deeply into the water. Be still and patient. Wait until some kind of answer rises – an image, metaphor, feeling, figure, place – whatever. Take your time. (30 seconds)

8. Reflect on what has been revealed. See how it might help you answer your question. Hold it dear. If nothing has come to you, save the image in your soul and wait for a revelation to come later on when the time is right. (15 seconds)

9. Now thank the beings who came to help you. Express your love and gratitude for their assistance as they now depart and feel their gratitude as well for the work you're doing on yourself and in the world. (10 seconds)

10. Find your way back to the present, this moment, and your normal experience of self and body, and when you're ready, open your eyes and get re-oriented to where we are. (5 seconds)

11. Finally, take a moment to reflect on your revelation. What does it mean to you?

12. Open your eyes and begin writing about what happened and what it means to you.

Moving from Calling to Response

Let's take this discernment process one more step. Here's a list of fifteen possible roles we could play in the world. They're in no particular order. As you read them, underline the ones that kindle your inner fire. Here they are. You could be a...

- *Climate warrior* defending Creation against the continuing assault of development, pollution, and exploitation through social protest and civil disobedience.
- *Citizen Lobbyist* pressuring local, state and national governments to declare a climate emergency and adopt immediate climate legislation
- *Gardener or Animal Lover* nourishing and supporting life in all its forms
- *Healer* of physical, emotional, mental or spiritual wounds in human and non-human beings, nurturing the hurt and broken back to life
- *Artist* expressing and welcoming the Spirit's powerful message of loving creativity through your own work. Art is the transformation of consciousness.
- *Lover of Creation* blessing every living thing with kindness, gratitude and praise
- *Skillful Builder for a Sustainable New World* as enlightened craftsman, engineer, laborer, farmer, planner, chef, inventor, lawyer or educator
- *Contemplative* immersed in prayer and unitive consciousness sending healing energies throughout Creation
- *Scientist*, professional or amateur, seeking to understand the nature and causes of climate damage and its repair
- *Spiritual Leader* creating or revitalizing sacred ritual, celebration and theology in service to Creation
- *Social Organizer* inspiring and mobilizing community planning for long-term local sustainability and immediate climate action.
- *Conflict Manager* skilled in compassionate non-violent communication and community problem-solving, guiding fractured groups through difficult choices toward unifying values and action
- *Volunteer* donating time, energy, skills, and money to political or climate action organizations

- *Nature Mystic* going outside and falling in love with Creation for continued support, inspiration, and motivation
- Last but not least, Reducer of your own Carbon Footprint through lifestyle changes and carbon offset programs. And remember, the word "sacrifice" comes from the Latin and means "to make sacred." What you give up helps restore the sacred world.

Look back at the roles you underlined. Write about what you discovered. What is that fire that flared up inside? Why was each role you picked especially exciting? Now write about how you might express these roles in the world. Don't make any immediate decisions, just witness what's coming to mind.

Conclusions

While we may engage all these roles in different degrees and combinations, each of us has been chosen, by temperament, passion, interest or soul, to help the world in a unique way. What have you begun to recognize as your own natural and unique gifts and its path of expression. For me, the answer was right under my nose but I kept thinking it had to lie elsewhere. What brings me alive, what can't I not do, where is my deep gladness, what touches my wounded heart? The answer was writing. I was doing it all along. I still can't seem to stop. A lifetime of education, professional training, therapy experience, spiritual practice and teaching, exploration of consciousness aging, and the pain I feel everywhere in the climate crisis, all continue to fill me with wonder, insight, and compassion, so I keep writing. May you find what is right under your nose as well.

Recommendations

1. Weave your pond images and chosen roles into a larger quilt of imagination. What do you see? How do you feel?

What calls you now?

2. Calling is often something you take for granted and overlook. Sometimes family and friends see it more clearly than you. Ask for feedback.

3. Try out your calling in small experiments and then review the results. If you're on your true path, you will begin to feel excitement and inspiration. Let it come.

Part III. The Mystical Journey in Apocalyptic Times

Conceiving this apocalyptic time in history as a clarion call to the spiritual journey can awaken new meaning and purpose in life no matter who or where you are. To that end, Part III presents a profound and powerful story that will engage your imagination, take you on a life-changing adventure, and bring you home with revelations to guide your new life. Before we embark, however, we need to understand the nature of mysticism.

Chapter 7

The Wonder of Mysticism: It's Not What You Think!

Mysticism has a negative reputation in western religion, often considered as irresponsible dabbling in the dark arts or defiance of church elders. But to understand this universal experience and its potential for healing a world in crisis, we need to distinguish between spirituality, religion, and mysticism, and appreciate the transformational powers of mystical consciousness and mystical activism.

Spirituality and Religion

As implied earlier, spirituality refers to the ultimate meaning we personally ascribe to our lives from our religious education, everyday experiences, and moments of sacred realization. In other words, our spirituality represents the individual conclusions we've reached so far about the nature and purpose of existence, God, morality and the universe. It's not surprising, therefore, that so many different spiritual beliefs exist – there are as many answers as people. In this regard, spirituality differs from religion. For example, a congregation of three hundred members will have one formal religion but three hundred unique spiritual interpretations of that religion. While religious scholars and teachers within a religion do debate its teachings, this merely reflects their individual spiritual viewpoints disguised as theological arguments. In sum, we always find the truths closest to our own heart and life circumstances. Spirituality may also serve as a stepping-stone from formal religion, with its history, scriptures, theology and practices, to personal experience of the divine, which leads me to mysticism.

Mysticism

Mysticism simply refers to the firsthand experience of the sacred. It's not weird, "woo woo," or far out. We've all had big or little mystical experiences, like the stunned amazement of meeting our newborn child for the first time, standing in silent awe gazing up at ancient redwood trees, falling in love for the first time and seeing the face of our beloved shining like an angel, feeling the palpable holiness of a sacred place, or simply being deeply present at the passing of a loved one. In these moments, the mind stops its chatter, perception heightens, the world transfigures in beauty, and we subtly experience the sacred consciousness that pervades Creation. Mystical Experience is a breakthrough of the divine into personal awareness that reveals the absolute sacredness of life.

Mystical Consciousness

Mystical consciousness arises from this same thought-free, sacred awareness, only now we learn to experience it intentionally, and I have created numerous exercises for awakening its power. In its fullness, mystical consciousness unveils the exquisitely beautiful, infinitely precious, luminous, and timeless reality known as Creation. We discover anew that everything is sacred, including us, for the divine has become the world and the world has become Creation.

Mystical Activism

Mystical activism evolves naturally from mystical consciousness for we now awaken a relationship with the divine as Creation itself. Do you want to experience God first hand? Experience Creation in mystical consciousness. This experience is profoundly motivating. Sensing the Beloved as nature, we respond with gratitude, amazement, wonder, awe and love. We begin to heal our relationship with the sacred world. We invite her guidance. And we fight to defend her. It's like finding a young child toddling across a busy street. We don't just drive by, we do whatever it takes to save that child. It's the same thing with Creation. In that moment of realization, we suddenly understand how sacred and precious all life is on Earth and we can't not respond.

Mysticism and the Earth Crisis

How does mysticism relate to our global nightmare? Here's the answer. Long ago we forgot our inborn mystical nature and abandoned Creation. We didn't get kicked out, we left on our own accord. Instead of witnessing Creation in mystical consciousness, our waking hours are now spent in artificially insulated environments separated from the natural world – cars, houses, offices, stores, and jobs; worse, our consciousness is totally consumed by TV, cell phones, head phones, video games, the Internet, news feeds, social media, endless conversations, and our own unruly chattering minds. We live almost entirely in our thoughts, beliefs, opinions and identities. We don't see the sacred world anymore! That's why it's in crisis. Creation has been suffering all around us for years and we haven't noticed. We've been too busy. Worse, failing to see the sacred nature of reality, we go on desecrating Creation, exploiting her as an endless supply of raw materials, a cash cow of new consumer products, or a garbage dump for toxic waste and discarded packaging. No wonder she is wounded and angry. Because we are so lost in thought, we desperately need to come home to the first-hand experience of the sacred as Creation.

The Challenge of Change

What we're facing in the global crisis is huge. It's going to require thousands of changes and a radical transformation of consciousness to survive. Personal or governmental goals can motivate us in the short run, but in the years and decades of this transition, and in the face of terrible losses, suffering and despair, we need something much more powerful to sustain us, and that something is the experience of the sacredness of life – not as a metaphor, cliché, symbol, happy sentiment in a Hallmark card – but as reality itself. We protect what we experience as sacred.

In mystical activism, we live more and more in the divine flow of here and now, and experience the sacred world in everything we do – raising our children, loving our family and our friends, performing our work, being kind and considerate, caring for community and environment, pursuing climate activism, and even the simplest human acts of eating, drinking and loving – they are all sacred in awakened perception. In this way, sacred consciousness reverberates throughout human activity, touching everyone, everything, everywhere, tipping the balance toward peace, healing, inclusiveness and joy.

Conclusions

Mysticism is an amazing resource. Equally astounding is how we kept it in the closet for so many centuries. We will soon discover that it is not only helpful, it may hold the key to transforming the world and our entire way of life. The mystical shift has long been coming. Let's find out what it's about.

Recommendations

1. Make a list of your own little or big mystical experiences. When did you feel especially close to the divine? Find a memory that touches you and describe how it still makes you feel. Reliving mystical moments will increase your ability to find and experience them now and in the future.

2. Ask others to share their mystical experiences with you. This sharing is not only fascinating, it activates a mystical consciousness between you. That is the future.

3. Imagine how differently your life would be if you lived

more and more in the flow of mystical consciousness. Describe this new kind of life in your journal and imagine bringing it alive. Use your intuition. What would it be like?

Chapter 8

The Birds Who Flew beyond Time: A Mystical Allegory

A modern retelling of the Sufi poem, *"The Conference of the Birds,"* by the thirteenth-century mystic Attar, this beautiful story, published in 2009 by Anne Baring and beautifully illustrated by Thetis Blacker, symbolically depicts the universal spiritual journey and, with great prescience, anticipates its profound relevance to our current global crisis. Though I recommend everyone read the story in its entirety, I retell it here in abbreviated form to provide a spiritual vision of the mystical work we can do in the coming months and years to rebuild a very broken world. It tells a difficult story and we must be ready for a difficult journey, for we are the birds and this is our story, too. Read this tale aloud, picture every scene, see the action, hear the sounds, smell the landscapes, and let it come alive in your imagination. Become one of the birds in this epic adventure.

Our story begins as thousands of birds from around the globe gather in a beautiful glen to receive a message from the Earth. She has called them together for a special announcement. The assembled throng chatter, gossip and jostle for room. "Why are we here?" "What does the Earth want for us?" When the birds settle down, the Earth begins, "I have called you here today to ask for your help. I am sick. My rivers are poisoned, my forests are dying, my air is polluted, my creatures are suffering, and humans kill each other with hate. Will you help me? Will you to take a long and difficult journey to save my life?"

A chattering-tweeting-screeching din swells in response to the Earth's shocking plea, fueled in no small degree by the birds' questions, doubts, fear and confusion. In the midst of this wild cacophony, a little Hoopoe bird lands on a tree stump in the center of the assembly and asks for silence. Finally, when all are still, she begins, "I am a messenger of the invisible realm and I will show you the way the Earth has proclaimed. Now, listen carefully. You must fly through seven dark and treacherous valleys. If you survive, you must then dive to the bottom of a mysterious sea, find the Great Being dwelling there in a beautiful garden, and bring back a message that might save the Earth's life." The Hoopoe further explains, "At the beginning of time, the Great Being planted a magic Golden Feather in each of your hearts. This sacred feather links you to each other and to the Great Being. But you forgot its original meaning and your feathers simply became a source of jealously and competition. But this feather is sacred. It will lead you to the Great Being. You must care for it with love and gratitude."

Bewildered by all this strange information and growing more fearful by the moment, the birds prattle on anxiously, making up countless excuses to decline the journey, "We would have to leave our special duties." "I might have to survive in a strange place." "Maybe this Hoopoe is exaggerating or dreaming." "It's just too dangerous." "It's probably too late to do any good anyway." Countering each excuse, the Hoopoe reminds them of the Golden Feather in their hearts, the Earth's deep suffering, and all the Great Being's love for them. Soothed by the Hoopoe's words, the birds finally agree to follow her on this strange and dangerous odyssey.

Now that she has the birds' commitment and full attention, the Hoopoe describes their arduous journey in more detail. "You will pass through seven dark valleys each controlled by a terrifying, powerful, and invisible monster. Once, long ago, these monsters were one with the Great Being but suffered deep and terrible wounds, causing them to forget this sacred relationship. Now they are only filled with hate. Although you will all go together, each of you must find your own way."

With the roar of thousands of fluttering wings, the birds rise into the air, darken the sky with their vast numbers, and set off on *their sacred quest led by the beautiful, multi-colored Hoopoe. Soon this great multitude of flying birds come to the first valley – the Valley of Doubt – and grow panicky. As they enter the valley, the birds begin to hear terrifying words that seem to come from within, whispering, "You are not good or smart enough to survive this journey. You will fail miserably." Now the birds' wings grow heavy with doubt and their weariness mounts. Finally, prompted by the Hoopoe to remember the Golden Feather and to trust themselves, most birds take heart and fly onward through the first valley, though some, believing the words inside are their own, give up and are left behind.*

The great flock continues onward and soon enters the second valley – the Valley of False Dreams – where the powerful monster offers them a delicious drink, promising that it will help them forget their fear and loneliness. "Here, take this, you will feel so much better and braver." Many birds are tempted, drink the drugged potion, and begin to fall asleep. Though nearly unconscious, they hear the far-off cry of the Hoopoe and fight valiantly to reach fresh air and regain consciousness; others, however, fall asleep and are left behind.

In the third valley – the Valley of Envy – evil, deceptive and seductive words whisper from within setting the birds against each other. Suddenly, each wants to be like another thought to be superior and, jockeying for this higher status, get tangled in nets of envy. Once again, those who hear the Hoopoe's inspiring call remember the Golden Feather break free; others are left behind with their bitter complaints and comparisons.

Upon entering the fourth valley – the Valley of Hate – powerful volcanos spew winds of fire that burn the birds' wings and the valley's monster roars terrifying threats of defeat and destruction. The birds quake with fear but again the brave Hoopoe calls out words of inspiration and they rally to resist this call of hatred and continue onward; sadly many already lie dead on the valley floor.

Next the birds come upon the fifth valley – the Valley of Power, a cold and desolate place. Fear strangles their hearts. The words from this arrogant and powerful monster tear apart the birds' hope and confidence, ranting, "You are too little, ignorant and weak to withstand my dominion." Once again, the tireless Hoopoe desperately calls to her birds to renew their hope and courage. The birds are also saved by clever ingenuity of their smallest companions, tiny birds who flock together to block the monster's spell, though many others turn to stone.

In the sixth valley – the Valley of Cruelty, the monster urges the remaining birds to be ruthless and spiteful. Wave upon wave of demonic creatures assault them from all sides, egging them on to choose a life of cruelty. A hawk, who has killed many in the past, suddenly recognizes his own cruelty and shouts, "I refuse the call to violence! I will forever be a warrior for life now." Remembering the holiness of the Great Being, the Hawk inspires his comrades to break the valley's spell. The battle is ferocious, many perish, but not all.

A small band of tired and tattered birds comes to the seventh and last valley – the Valley of Despair – where the monster's words, spoken as if from within, try to convince them that the journey is hopeless. It whispers, "There is no garden, there is no Great Being, and there is no message. Give up. Go back while you still can." To break this final soul-crushing spell, the Hoopoe mysteriously instructs her birds, "Close your eyes and you will see a beam of light. It will lead you directly to the Great Being. Follow it. You will not be disappointed." With new hope, and compassionately recalling the Earth's tragic plight, the birds again take heart and follow the beam, all the while singing out their love for Creation and trust in the Great Being. Miraculously, even the valley's monster joins the song.

Weary and winnowed in number, the last birds arrive at the end of time and the edge of a strange sea. Though terribly afraid of drowning, they bravely follow the skillful paradise kingfisher and dive into the water, deeper and deeper, searching for the prophesized garden and Great Being at the bottom. They descend through strangely buoyant crystal-clear waters, and just when they can go no further, the birds arrive at the most beautiful place they have ever seen. There, before them, stands the "House of the Treasure" where the "Keeper of the Door" tests their sincerity with questions and then invites them into the heart of the Great Being – a room of "a thousand dazzling mirrors" that reveals "the innermost secret of Creation." At that moment, they see through the "hundred thousand veils" and experience themselves as both the Great Being and existence itself, at one and the same time.

The Great Being now addresses the handful of surviving birds. Its words magically illuminate the Golden Feather in each heart. Then, turning to the message they must bring back to Earth, the Great Being explains,

> *You yourselves, as you are now, you are the message. You have broken the spells of the monsters of the seven valleys... Now you know your true nature, the divine heart of your being. You know I am the heart of each one of you and you are within my Heart forever. Now you can return to Earth knowing that every atom, every stone, every leaf, every tree of Earth is lit with the one secret, blazing light that streams from me. Wherever you are, you have only to imagine me and I will be with you. If ever you are anxious, I will give you strength and wisdom. If ever you are afraid, you have only to imagine my light and it will stand shining before you. You have flown beyond the edge of time so you know there is no death but only one eternal life. Tell all the children of the Earth what you have seen so they will not fear death. Go now, my beloved Birds, and tell your story to the Earth. (Baring, pp. 37–39)*

With their health and plumage magically restored, the birds rise gracefully together and fly toward home. The trip home seems to flash by in a second. On the way, they notice that the valleys are transfigured and restored in astounding beauty. Even their lost comrades return to life. Arriving home safely, the birds are greeted by those they left behind and a great celebration erupts. With immense gratitude, the Earth thanks her birds and says,

> *You are my special messengers: tell your story to my children. If they listen to your voice in their hearts, they will know what to do for me. They will love and protect me for my sake and for the sake of their children and their children's children. They will not fall under the spell of the seven monsters. One day, each of them will make the journey to the garden in the depths of the sea. And you will be their guide as the Hoopoe was your guide. You will lead them to the House of the Treasure and the Great Being who is the life of all life. Like the Hoopoe, you now are the messengers of the world invisible, and the Golden Flower will shine forever in your hearts. (Baring, p. 39).*

Take a deep breath. Settle back in your seats. Let the story marinate your heart. You know its deep. When you're ready, read on to unveil the story's mystical symbolism.

Understanding the Story's Symbolism

Of course, we are the birds in this prophetic story and Earth is asking us to take the same journey, find the same Great Being, and bring home a message that can save the whole living world. And like the birds, we have no idea in the beginning what this journey involves or what we are supposed to do. Does that sound familiar? This is our dilemma, too. What does the spiritual journey have to do with saving the world?

The Birds Who Flew beyond Time is an allegorical description of the mystical journey we each take seeking help from the Great Being – God, the Holy One, Divinity, Allah, Yahweh, use whatever name you love. It is a journey into the sacred heart of Creation. We seek it in prayer, meditation, sacred rituals, wilderness time, and mystical states. To reach this realm, we, too, must overcome self-centered excuses, cynical or hopeless whispers, and descend deep within until we dissolve sacred consciousness and awaken its transformed perception. This is a description of the universal spiritual journey! However, this journey is not easy and few succeed because we are taught to value thought, reason and conversation over the mental silence and stillness of divine consciousness. We choose chatter over awakened consciousness. But that's what spiritual practices are for – to reach a state of emptiness that opens into divine consciousness. It also follows that, though we can travel together, no one can do this for you. But what does that mean for us?

Beginning the Journey

As in the story, we must each first pass through the seven valleys that block our path to the Great Being. Below are the seven valleys and the whispers we might hear in each. In each valley, ask yourself two questions, "Are these my whispers?" and "Is this the valley I am most stuck in?" See if you can identify the words of your own inner monster. Here we go…

1. *Valley of Doubt:* "This situation is not going to be so bad." "I don't really see it happening anyway." "Most people don't get that sick from the virus." "So the Earth's a little warmer, big deal – summertime everywhere!" "This whole thing is getting totally exaggerated" and "What could one person do anyway?" "Ah, forget it. People are just getting too worked up!" Do any of these whispers sound familiar?

2. *Valley of False Dreams:* "Science or someone else will save us." "With so many smart people working on these problems, there's going to be plenty of solutions." "In the meantime, I'll keep busy with TV, my favorite novel, shopping, or playing online, and wait until it's fixed." "This is actually a good thing, you'll see." Do any of these

whispers sound familiar?

3. *Valley of Envy:* "I know rich people who have way more money than me so they'll survive better, it's not fair." "I envy old people who will die naturally and not have to face any of these big problems." "Young people don't get very sick. Why me?" "I'm important, I'm rich, I'm smart. Envy me!" "Look at me, I don't use plastic straws anymore!" Do any of these whispers sound familiar?

4. *Valley of Hate:* "I hate people who make me feel frightened or guilty." "I hate people who are trying to take what's mine – immigrants!" "I hate people exaggerating all this and trying to scare me." "I hate the government – they don't care about us." "I hate the rich, they have it all." Do any of these whispers sound familiar?

5. *Valley of Power:* "If I align with powerful people, we can control food, water and other resources." "We can build our own walls and keep others out." "We have guns, we'll take what we need." "I am superior, I am always right, I know everything. Don't mess with me!" Do any of these whispers sound familiar?

6. *Valley of Cruelty:* "The weak deserve what they get." "It's a dog-eat-dog world." "Hey, if you're not prepared, it's your problem." "I don't talk to stupid people." "Get off my land." Do any of these whispers sound familiar?

7. *Valley of Despair:* "It's hopeless." "It's overwhelming, there's nothing we can really do to make a difference." "It's already too late, we're going to die anyway." "What's the point of trying?" "I just want to die quickly." "I'm too old to fight." Do any of these whispers sound familiar?

Go back and underline the phrases that sound like your whispers. Add any other phrases I've missed. Now identify the valley you're most stuck in. Why does it have so much control over you? Explore this question in our journal or with friends.

Unless we face our own denial and avoidance, we will never experience the secret of Creation and save humanity. But what is that secret?

The second part of the story holds the secret that can heal Creation. After passing through the seven valleys of disbelief, the birds arrive at a place "that lies east of the sun and west of the moon, over the edge of time, and beyond the seven valleys; the place that is neither here nor there but everywhere." These words beautifully describe mystical consciousness – timeless, omnipresent, ineffable, mysterious and uncharted. There we meet the Great Being and awaken the experience of the divine Self – the Golden Feather. We also discover the divine world – the sacred Garden and its extension as Creation itself. These revelations lead to "the innermost secret of creation..."

Remember how the Great Being described Creation: "every atom, every stone, every leaf, every tree of Earth is lit with the one secret, blazing light that streams from me." Creation is the natural world infused with holiness. In this mystical state, we, the Great Being, and Creation, are all one, no boundaries. Suddenly we understand the Great Being's message: To save Creation, we must *experience* this mystical unity and share it with others. Creation still exists. It's everywhere. It's here now. It's us. It's God. It's the world. Its love streams through every tree, rock, ant, breeze, dark night and sunny day. Now everything changes. We are Creation. We are the lover, the beloved, and the love. We are the realization that can save the world. Moved by direct contact with the source of all, we work tirelessly to save the divine manifestation that is our sacred Earth.

If Creation is sacred, what about the coronavirus, global warming, over-population and the civilization's unraveling? Are they sacred, too? Let's start by reminding ourselves that we are not planetary VIPs. We are not the only sacred beings in Creation. We need to belong to Creation, not rule it. The human thread is only one in an infinitely complex fabric woven by the sacred loom. More fundamentally, we need to realize that the world is not what we think. Thought creates duality, replacing the direct perception of "what is" with what we *think* it is. When we stop thinking, heighten awareness, and experience the world without preconceived ideas and labels, we find a mystery very different than we thought. By analogy, reading about swimming completely misses the transformational experience of stepping into the water. Because this is a sacred question, the ultimate answer can only be found in sacred consciousness, and then it will be so obvious you will laugh out loud.

Conclusions

When confronted with a profound or distressing dilemma, unsolvable by conventional means, we instinctively turn to the sacred. We sense that reaching out to the divine, and experiencing its mystical Presence, can reveal an answer we have been missing. But, gripped by fear, immaturity, and old wounds, we resist the journey. We turn away. We rationalize our reluctance. We want to stay in control, keep the power, take the credit, and do it alone. *The Birds Who Flew beyond Time* reminds us that the spiritual path invites us instead to surrender our defensive hubris, independence, and separate self, and experience the transformation of mystical consciousness. The journey is into the mystical.

Recommendations

1. Look again at the valley that arrested your consciousness. Have you broken free of its dismissive whispers? If not, what do you need to do to unlock its chains?
2. Retell this story in your own words. Then retell it as your own story, imagining how you might experience the Great Being's revelations. How differently would you live if you experienced the world as divine?
3. Learn more about mystical experience and mystical

consciousness. An open door into enlightenment, this state that will transform your consciousness and light your way through the dark valleys of this apocalypse into the always-new experience of Creation.

Chapter 9

Finding Our Soul's Mission in Scary Times: It's Why We're Here

Why am I here? What did I come here to do? And how do these questions relate to the Great Being's revelation? It's time now to look at the ultimate source of our work: the soul's chosen mission.

Understanding the Soul's Mission

Malidoma Somé, an initiated West African shaman with a western Ph.D., talked about soul-work one day in a Mendocino Men's Gathering years ago. He explained that in his culture's cosmology, spiritual elders in the pre-life realm meet with each soul planning a return to Earth to help them choose their purpose in coming back. Once an appropriate task is identified, the individual is sent forth to be reborn but soon forgets the plan. At some point along the road of life, an inner clock starts ticking and restlessness ensues because the individual unconsciously knows that their soul's work is still undone. This disquiet arises in each of us. It's meant to draw attention to the unfinished work of the soul. Finding our purpose in life, therefore, is about remembering why we came and discerning what this soul-work is right now. Whatever your religious or spiritual beliefs, Malidoma's explanation represents an archetypal description of the soul's calling. Here's a personal example.

At the callow age of 14, I underwent open-heart surgery for the correction of a congenital atrial-septal defect. The operation saved my life but nearly obliterated my soul, for during surgery, I woke up feeling hands working inside my heart. It's called anesthesia awareness and happens when anesthesia levels fall too low to maintain unconsciousness while paralyzing neuromuscular blocking agents preventing the patient from communicating this horror to medical staff. I repressed this horrific trauma for decades until a defibrillating shock administered to convert a heart arrhythmia shattered my defenses and I was forced to relive the devastating power of the surgery. I broke. Unable to hold the emotional pain of others, I gave up my work as a clinical psychologist and returned to school for a doctorate in interfaith spirituality. Yet all the while, I kept wondering – and asking! – why must I suffer this immense anguish only to lose my professional identity, career, income, and psychological community. At the culmination of my studies, however, I began writing and seven books poured forth articulating the surprising spiritual realizations I came here to share. Thank you, Malidoma!

Discovering the Soul's Mission in Disappointment and Loss

If I had kept trying to return to my career – and believe me I tried for a long time, more depression would have followed, for depression often signals the betrayal of soul. It was time for my soul to move on. Gradually, I understood that my childhood trauma represented an unfinished adolescent initiation. The initiation was incomplete because it lacked the ritual structure, sacred purpose, personal consciousness, and community participation required to unveil my soul's deep calling and unique gifts. Absent this sacred container, and to protect my fragile childhood ego, the revelation fell instead into the darkness of the unconscious. Forty years later, with the clock ticking loudly, it was time to uncover my soul's mission and its vision. In this fashion, the personal discovery of our mission often requires many disappointments and losses, bringing the issue up over and over until we finally pay attention to the call of soul. Sometimes it takes a really big crisis – like the one we are in now – to find what your mission wants you to do.

Tools for Beginning the Search

What is your soul's prearranged assignment in the global crisis? The answer, of course, is deeply personal. Because only you can answer this question, here are some tools for uncovering your sacred mission.

Create Your Own Spiritual Retreat. For example, if you are in self-quarantine, treat it as a spiritual retreat. Rather than constituting a prison of interminable boredom, consider it an opportunity to reflect on the work of your soul. Happily, there are many ways to do this – we can meditate, pray, dwell in deep silence, write in our journal, analyze dreams, consult the Tarot or I Ching, read the great spiritual writers, consult or teleconference with a therapist or spiritual director, or initiate creative phone discussions with close friends. While you pursue revelations, keep asking this mantra-like question, "What is my soul's mission in this time and place?" It will come. But keep in mind, revelations mature like newly-planted bulbs so clear the weeds of everyday distractions and misleading beliefs to make room for new growth. And when government-mandated quarantines end, let this kind of personal spiritual retreat become a weekly spiritual practice akin to the Jewish Sabbath. It need never lose its mystical dimension or its capacity to nourish our spiritual growth.

Access Your Soul's Mission Directly. You can also access your soul's mission more directly. Try this exercise.

Pick a spiritual question that appeals to you from the list below, write a spontaneous answer (don't censure anything, just free associate), then ask the same question again and write another answer. Keep repeating this process for several minutes. You may end up with as many as 5, 10 or even 20 responses. When no more new answers arise, review your responses, underline the ones that feel most authentic, and write about what you are learning. Then repeat the exercise with another question. Here are the questions. Add your own questions later if you wish.

What did I come here to do?
What is my soul's mission in this crisis?
What is the nature of my soul?
What is an image or symbol of my soul mission?
Where or when have I felt my mission before?

This exercise is like digging a hole deeper and deeper into the psyche until we reach the "House of the Treasure" and the revelations of the Great Being. Trust what comes up this treasure hunt. Carry it around inside. See how each revelation feels until you sense the most important one of all.

Dialogue with Your Soul. Here is another exercise – a simple but powerful visualization process for meeting your soul and asking directly for its guidance. Find a comfortable spot to sit, have paper and pen handy, clear your mind and follow these steps:

1. Imagine that you can see your soul somewhere in the room. Take your time. Let his or her image spontaneously come to you. Where is he or she standing or sitting?
2. Let the image become clearer. What does your soul look like? Start writing. Describe his or her physical appearance, clothes, age, facial expression, mood, attitude and emotional energy. Let the vision become clearer little by little, as if adjusting the lens on binoculars to bring the image into focus.
3. Verbally welcome your soul in whatever way you like. How does your soul respond to your reaching out?
4. Now begin writing a dialogue. You might start by saying how you feel, what's on your mind, or asking a question. When you've expressed yourself, sense the soul's energy

and imagine its response. Like spontaneous fantasy, let the conversation just take off. Record the dialogue without censoring or judging it.

5. Continue in this fashion pursuing any topics that are important to you. Consider asking if your soul's mission involves new learning, caring for others, making amends, awakening latent interests or aptitudes, or pursuing additional spiritual growth and transcendence. You will know the dialogue is authentic if your soul responds in ways that surprise you, provide new ideas or teaching, or affect you emotionally. The soul's vision always provides new information.

6. You may also find your soul being more assertive than you would have expected, pushing you to express your mission in the world. When the dialogue feels complete or runs out of gas, stop, thank your soul, say goodbye until next time, and reflect on what happened.

As you reread your dialogue, write your reflections. What did you learn? How do you feel? What was your soul's essential message to you?

Conclusions

Reliving my heart trauma triggered a personal apocalypse but it wasn't my ending; rather it unearthed the universal symbolism of death and rebirth – the death of my old life and the birth of a new one powered by a pre-agreed mission ticking in my psyche. I can now imagine the conversation I had with my ancestors and elders in the pre-life. With their blessing, I brought wisdom from the Great Being to share in this life but didn't find it until all else failed and I collapsed into the darkness of defeat. I believe this kind of transition is far more common than we realize. So, why are you here? What did you come here to do? And will your soul's mission help you rise to the challenge of these catastrophic times? As problems multiply may you rediscover your sacred mission and help humanity find its new life. Let me know what you discover.

Recommendations

1. Can you recall a previous time when your life fell apart? Could it be that your soul arranged this collapse to change your direction? How? What are your intuitions?

2. Perhaps our soul is like the Hoopoe, leading us in times of crisis, into the divine mystery to receive a sacred message, and perhaps this book is like the journey meant to awaken your own revelations.

3. What would you like to say to your spiritual elders were you to meet again on the other side? Did you do what you came to do? How?

Part IV. A Cosmic Story

As we near the end of our journey, ask yourself, "What have I learned so far?" "Has my perspective changed?" "Have hope, purpose, meaning, determination and community replenished my soul for the coming struggle?" "Have I grown in spiritual or mystical understanding?" Noticing our own evolution integrates our answers into our daily life and spiritual practice.

Here are my hopes for you. I hope you have discovered the wealth of experience, courage, and love you have inside, the personal gifts you've earned in completing the tasks of aging, and hints of the mission your soul has chosen to serve the world. I hope you now feel more prepared to survive and sometimes even thrive in this global crisis, not only for your own sake, but for our children, grandchildren, and future generations. As seasoned elders, we know the way is dark and dangerous, but we have come through hard times before and, with a little help from our friends, we can choose to go on. To that end, this final section places our collective "Dark Night of the Soul" in a cosmic and evolutionary perspective. If we trust that the divine universe is a work in progress, a conscious and unfolding miracle, perhaps we can trust ourselves to embody it and light the way for others.

Chapter 10

The Labor and Birth of a New Humanity: The Blossom that Opens with Pain

Archetypal psychology, world mythology, and mystical revelation have long suggested that human culture evolves in an ancient and recurring cycle of four stages, beginning with a sacred vision of Creation, its subsequent corruption and exploitation by the ego, the consequent collapse of civilization, and humanity's spiritual rebirth amidst the rubble.

Our current global crisis may represent the bill of sale for the anthropocentrism, cultural greed and superficiality, and the political venality of this latest round of civilization. The accumulated karma of human history breaks over us like a great silent tidal wave, portending vast human and wildlife suffering in its wake. Yet recognizing this age-old spiritual cycle, we can also sense something deeper if we try, something transpersonal, metaphysical, other worldly, supernatural, divine, mystical, transformational, evolutionary, irreversible, supernal, necessary, awe-full, and reality-shifting. While words fail me here, the spiritual intuition resonates nonetheless – a visionary transformation is at hand.

Humanity stands at the threshold of a *kairos* moment still imprisoned in a *chronos* mind. Kairos, referring to a breakthrough of divinity transcending time and place, is constantly overridden by our slavish devotion to the chronos order of clock and calendar time. What can we expect from such a transformational moment? While it can take many forms, the perceptive observer may notice these commonalities – panic and despair interrupt business-as-usual, chronos time and its calendar cease to be relevant, the old-world order disappears, mystical intuitions and revelations replaces self-centered thought, and divinity awakens consciousness to transfigure our perceptions of each other and the world. While this is indeed a life-threatening emergency in conventional consciousness; in sacred awareness, its purpose may be to unveil a radically new world, for apocalypse means revelation.

Now here's an intriguing idea. I believe that the symbolism of human pregnancy, labor and birth informs this apocalyptic time. What are the similarities? For most of us, the human process of conception and birth feel huge, prescient and uncontrollable; we sense mysterious forces acting within and without; and the culmination of this process changes our lives forever. Knowing things can go wrong, we prepare for anything, but in the end, we must trust the implicit purpose of pregnancy itself. These dimensions inform the Earth crisis, too. More than a metaphor, our planetary emergency signals a cosmic, divinely-transmuting miracle, profoundly feminine in nature, planting seeds of transformation in the inner darkness of the human psyche, and bringing forth a fresh new consciousness, achieved through blood and pain, yet in the end scrubbed clean of ugliness and corruption. In short, a new beginning.

The New Blossom

Beautifully describing the birth of her first child, Laura Weldon, Ohio Poet of the Year for 2019, wrote, "Childbirth taught me it is possible to understand pain." She recalled,

> *Labor with my first child progressed very slowly. All night I centered myself through contractions by staring at a chosen focal point – my husband's green eyes. At 22, I had no friends who were pregnant or had given birth. What I knew came from books and childbirth classes. I'd found the only doctor in our area who practiced the gentle natural birthing method known as Leboyer. He was a gruff elderly gentleman who reluctantly snuffed out his cigarette when I objected to it during my first office visit. I'd been*

told by another obstetrician I was certain to require a cesarean section because I was too petite. Yet here I was mentally celebrating as labor intensified because it meant I'd soon meet my child. I barely noticed the birthing room's white walls and its large black-rimmed clock. All my attention went to picturing the pain as urging a blossom open. In the morning a red-haired boy emerged weighing 9 pounds, 10 ounces.

All day I felt euphoric. It was revelatory to hold this new being. I wanted to do nothing but return his long liquid gaze. My own discomfort and hunger seemed irrelevant. That night as I held my baby, unable to sleep from wonderment, I heard the cries of a woman laboring in a nearby room. Perhaps it could be blamed on exhaustion or hormones, but for a moment the walls evaporated and I was with her, sharing her effort. Then time itself evaporated and I was with every woman who had labored to bring forth each previous generation, all the way from the beginning. Their struggle, their strength echoed in my own body. I could feel this resonate in the atoms making up every body ever formed. The moment ended but the feeling didn't. I had never used drugs but afterward I was high for days.

At this moment of humanity's new birth, we are equally unprepared for the necessary, powerful and painful contractions. Young, inexperienced in visionary transformations, attended by callow mates and gruff teachers, full of fear yet giddy with hope, we, too, seek to transmute our collective pain by urging the blossom open, ultimately rewarded with unexpected euphoria, the grace-filled miracle of tender new beginnings, the loving embrace of motherhood, deep compassion for the epic struggle of all life to survive, and numinous revelations of beauty, creativity, and cosmic abundance that arrive as we enter again the sacred dimension of being.

But it's rarely easy. When my daughter called to say she was pregnant for the first time, I was euphoric. More than that, I felt pregnant. I sensed a new life growing inside me as well and, unable to contain my joy, I danced crazily around the kitchen. And a new world was indeed born, though my daughter almost died in postpartum complications. We cannot minimize the possibilities of real suffering in this global transformation nor should we, but if we cling to the past, we will surely be lost.

A Fuller Revelation?

Mystics, poets, writers and artists remind us that the world is already sacred. In their awakened perception, they describe an exquisitely beautiful and enchanted world, lit from within, the divine essence and substance of all being – the essential message the Great Being gave the birds. They insist that if we look deeply, intensely, in thought-free sacred consciousness, we, too, will discover the living divine fabric of existence hiding beneath the mental world we project over Creation. Revelation always removes the filters of thought and belief to reveal the divine ground of being, and there will be much more revelation to come this transitional time. Faced with the possibility of extinction, our revelations will be equally profound. We prepare in hallowed expectation.

Along the path to a new awareness of Creation, we may have to surrender our attachments to the illusions and unsustainable conveniences of the "modern" world – self-importance, political arrogance, undeserved wealth, endless food in grocery stores, always accessible medical care, gas on every corner, upward mobility, ocean cruises and air travel. Recalling that sacrifice means *to make sacred* in Latin, we understand that great revelation follows great loss.

But likening her birth experience to our apocalyptic times, Laura also observed, "The pain we are undergoing, relentless as any mother's labor, may very well be urging a blossom open. This struggle and the strength required to get through it has been present each time history contracted, expanded, birthed a better reality." While the unveiling of Creation has already begun, we must be its midwives and receive it tenderly in our loving hands.

Conclusions

The labor and birth of a new human consciousness is more than a metaphor. This intuition forecasts a breakthrough of cosmic consciousness, but this time, a profoundly feminine one, missing for centuries in the patriarchal worldview. Loving, maternal, inclusive, natural, non-competitive, and non-hierarchical, this crisis may be the collective blossom of our time. The old world will die, a new one revealed, and our spiritual evolution will continue onward. And, as the Great Being explained, each of us now assumes the role of the Hoopoe; we must bring this revelation to the young. Put another way, humanity's new birth holds the promise of a new savior, who we will eventually discover is you and me.

Now is the moment of humanity's greatest step forward or final step into extinction. We stand in the fires of our own individual and cultural transformation. It doesn't matter what your personal history was or how you lived, this new birth will redeem and renew the life you chose to serve the world, if you're willing. Like all sacraments, this birth, too, is sacred. Indeed, the global crisis is humanity's own sacrament – personal, collective, and planetary. The angels watch in fear and hope. This is not the punishment of an authoritarian male God, it is the return of the deeply feminine power of unconditional love, offering at long last the sacred marriage of masculine and feminine, human and divine, Heaven and Earth. But it's up to us.

Recommendations

1. How might your life be reborn in this time? Can you catch a glimpse of its new blossom? As imagination prepares us for manifestation, begin to see into your future.
2. If we understand this global nightmare as divine

revelation, perhaps we'll find the courage, trust and inspiration we need to go on. What do you imagine the divine asking of us?

3. Reflect on the movement away from a patriarchal hierarchy to a more feminine and balanced culture. Can you sense how much we need this shift? Imagine living from an Earth-centered feminine consciousness. How might you begin to live like that now?

Chapter 11

New Consciousness, New Creation: It's Where We're Going

The new blossom of consciousness described in the last chapter has two dimensions – humanity's collective awakening and its central realization that Creation represents a mystical encounter with the divine. We are on the cutting edge of change now, where transformation leads to transfiguration.

Humanity's New Consciousness

Abraham Maslow, the father of humanistic psychology – the "Third Force" of American psychology, and its wonderfully enlivening concepts – "hierarchy of needs," "peak experiences," "self-actualizing personality," suffered a severe heart attack in his early sixties and died several months later. In the intervening months, a time of very fragile health he called his "post-mortem life," Maslow's personality changed dramatically, shifting from a nearly workaholic level of ambition and productivity to a steady state of transcendent calm, characterized by a deep serenity, unitive consciousness, spontaneous spiritual insights, and pervasive perceptions of radiance, beauty, and the miraculous nature of being. He called this new state of consciousness the *"plateau experience"* and said he could awaken it voluntarily and remain "turned on."

Pierre de Chardin, the French philosopher, paleontologist, Catholic priest, and mystic, coined the term "noosphere" to describe what he sensed as an emerging collective level of unity consciousness, a superintelligence infusing all of us with transhuman awareness and intelligence. Spiritual writer Aldous Huxley, too, suggested that an awakened intelligence was coming that would allow humans to transcend their individuality, accelerating the curve of spiritual evolution. I believe Maslow, de Chardin, and Huxley were describing an enduring state of mystical consciousness that will evolve one day for all of us, transforming our lives, our work, and our world.

As a mystic, I sense the potential for "plateau" consciousness emerging in these catastrophic times, but its full realization is up to us – like the birds, we must each take responsibility for our awakening if we are to serve humanity's transformation. This global apocalypse represents a major turning point in human civilization, moving us from the sins of greed, power, and patriarchy, to the all-infusing love and unity of divine consciousness, if we follow the inner light. Such is our collective mission.

But here is a surprising and hopeful truth: Crises awaken mystical consciousness, evoking the same intense, wide awake, "Oh my God!" here-and-now awareness that returns us to the immediate sensory present. We let go of beliefs, schedules, life goals, identities, retirement portfolios, or political views and return to the timeless unity consciousness of the divine. We can find countless examples of this principle, as during motor vehicle accidents when time suddenly slows down and consciousness profoundly sharpens perception, in the accelerated life review experienced by mountain climbers during accidental free fall, in a soldier's unplanned heroism transcending personal preoccupations to save another, and in all manner of Near-Death Experiences where dying is reconceived as a profound religious process. In these crisis-related altered states, the insecure little self falls away and we experience the awakening of consciousness and the power of love that invite a new kind of being, one infused with the sacred Presence. As Rachel Naomi Remen observes, "The daily fabric that covers what is most real is commonly mistaken for what is most real until something tears a hole in it and reveals the true nature of the world." As the Great Being revealed, "Now you can return to Earth knowing that every atom, every stone, every leaf, every tree of Earth is lit with the one secret, blazing light that streams from me."

The breakdown of civilization represents an opportunity to return to our original consciousness. When our house burns down or a tsunami destroys our village, we hold onto each other, our family, pets and livestock, and do whatever we can for each other. Because emergency consciousness and mystical consciousness are the same thing – one of the greatest paradoxes on the spiritual journey – crises bring profound opportunities for awakening. In the moment of crisis, we can literally step into God's consciousness and act from a divine flow of love and compassion. We become God in action. The primary enemies, of course, are the usual suspects –falling back into catastrophic thinking, turning against each other, or losing hope. We walk the razor's edge.

Coming Home to Creation

The ultimate healing step in this transition involves opening our hearts to Creation. Theologian Matthew Fox tells us, "An absence of the sense of the sacred is the basic flaw in many of our efforts at ecologically or environmentally adjusting our human presence to the natural world..." He adds, "More than ever, then, we need to stop and sit and be present ... allow our love for the world and the world's love for us to be deeply felt. This can carry us beyond nationhood and ethnic or racial or religious smallness into the much bigger world of creation itself. Love will be the source of our energy and of our imaginations that will render us effective agents for deeper change. Not superficial change, but a change that begins and ends with the reverence and gratitude we all carry in our hearts toward the universe that has birthed us. With that kind of deeper perspective, our prophetic callings stand a better chance of effective results." These words are a beautiful description of Mystical Activism – living in the flow of sacred conscious to serve the world right where we are.

Fox is hardly alone in this call to sacred awareness. Joanna Macy, a long time Earth activist and climate prophet, says, "While the truth that we are headed toward extinction is a terrible shock, it has the potential to quicken our collective awakening, powering a profound transformation of our world. This transformation begins within." And now carefully regard her next words for they are profoundly mystical, "We need to know ourselves, not only as individuals, but as co-creators within a deeply ensouled web of life where all is conscious. Once we align with the reality and depth intelligence of consciousness itself, we connect with a spiritual and moral power that gifts intuitive wisdom, guidance, and courage.... In essence, we are awakening into the profound intimacy of all things, where we directly know that all beings, nature, the earth, and the cosmos are a part of ourselves." This, too, is Mystical Activism – the awareness of the deep and sacred unity of conscious being.

Lastly, we turn to cultural historian, Thomas Berry, a profound and visionary thinker on ecological spirituality, the universe story. Berry writes,

Perhaps a new revelatory experience is taking place, an experience wherein human consciousness awakens to the grandeur and sacred quality of the Earth process. Humanity has seldom participated in such a vision since shamanic times, but in such a renewal lies our hope for the future for ourselves and for the entire planet on which we live.

Berry also has something to say about how we recover the sense of the sacred, explaining,

We will recover our sense of wonder and our sense of the sacred only if we appreciate the universe beyond ourselves as a revelatory experience of that numinous presence whence all things come into being. Indeed, the universe is the primary sacred reality. We become

sacred by our participation in this more sublime dimension of the world about us.

Berry's words are a prophetic, elegant, and sublime description of how experiencing the divine world can transform our lives and awaken Mystical Activism.

Recommendations

1. Have you noticed shifts in your own consciousness, where it seems as if the timeless mystery of eternity was somehow leaking into your own awareness? Have you noticed a dissolution of time's importance in your life so that clock, day-planner and date no longer matter so much? These are changes hinting at the coming mystical consciousness. What other changes do you notice?

2. Can you imagine acting in the moment, responding naturally and spontaneously to mystical awareness of "what is"? This is the shift from doing to being that comes in awakened aging. Spend one minute in a thought-free state of consciousness and see how differently your behavior arises.

3. In a divine world, Creation is a living, breathing, communicating being. Go outside and ask her how she feels and what she needs.

Chapter 12

Tying It All Together: Coming Home to Ourselves

Headings from the Table of Contents deliver the essential message of *Resilience: Aging with Vision, Hope, and Courage in a Time of Crisis*. Part I, "Aging in a Time of Crisis," reveals a new you facing humanity's biggest storm. "The Good News" is that aging has transformed us and "We Now Bear Gifts from the Tree of Life" to face hard times. "The Bad News" is that the "The Approaching Storm Is Huge." In Part II, "Practical Guidance for Survival," we learn that "Coping with Overwhelming Emotions" is critical and that we need to prepare by "Shoring Up Our Resources" and that asking, "How Can I Help?"

What came next, however, must have been a little surprising. Part III, "The Mystical Journey in Apocalyptic Times" shares "The Wonders of Mysticism," and "A Mystical Allegory of Awakening," We realize that the Earth is calling us to take a mystical journey through the valleys of our own denial and resistance to meet the Great Being within and awaken the ultimate solution to our problems. For mystics, this journey is the purpose of life and the essence of spiritual practice, culminating in the ultimate healing revelation: Sacred Creation. With this awakening, we begin "Finding the Soul's Mission in Scary Times." Part IV. "A Cosmic Story," describes the mystical "The Labor and Birth of a New Humanity" and the coming of a "New Consciousness, New Creation."

It's been quite a journey! As mystics, mythologists, and depth psychologists will recognize, this book was born from a timeless archetypal vision that each generation must learn anew. For our over-65 demographic, however, it is a time for realizing that vision – understanding it, living it, acting from its essential realization, and bringing the message home to those who follow and to the future. As the journey of life always returns to its beginning, we return to the theme in Chapter 1: We're Resilient, Brand New, and Still Growing.

I close with one last revelation. Our collective response to the coronavirus has demonstrated how quickly we can change as a society when confronted with a massive threat. We have not only adapted our behavior to reduce the danger, but we have also returned to the sacred and eternal values of creativity, community, love and Creation. Meanwhile, an even larger threat is growing – think climate change, the population explosion, and the unraveling of civilization. But the world is mobilizing and our generation brings a lifetime of wisdom and a new consciousness to humanity's great work. Let us travel together to answer the Earth's call.

Recommendations

1. Further transform your experience of Creation in mystical consciousness. Tune into every living and nonliving being, and sense the Great Being's light streaming through it, infusing Creation with divine consciousness. Make this a spiritual practice that brings you home to Creation consciousness. Then Creation will show you what it needs to heal.

2. Imagine a Creation-friendly conscious community. How would we relate to each other? How would we supply our basic needs for food, shelter, health and safety? Share your ideas with others to begin weaving a common vision.

3. How has your heart been touched by themes and revelations of this book? What fires now stir in your soul. Where do you want to do your Mystical Activism?

Final Words and a Prayer

I want to close this book with simple words and a prayer.

This is the most exquisite moment on Earth. We all need to fall in love again with what is.... Is anything sweeter than being with the mother in her suffering?
Joanna Macy

A Prayer for Mystical Activists

Divine Consciousness of Life, Earth and Cosmos, God of all names and none, holy Presence dwelling in every creature, we come to you on our knees, in guilt and shame, in sorrow and dread, admitting horrific crimes against Creation. Listening to Earth's dying cries, we acknowledge our sins of arrogance, apathy, selfishness, plunder and rape. Our "stewardship" of Creation has been a tragic joke. In failure and profound remorse, we humbly seek forgiveness and guidance – we have completely lost our way and stand to lose so much more.

We know you, Divine One. We share your Being and Consciousness. We are you when we cease pretending to be someone else, someone separate and superior, someone in charge. In abject surrender, in ego-shattering fear and grief, in naked helplessness, we seek the only path home: we return to you. As the fires and storms of human foolishness consume our grandiosity and our world, we ask you to receive us, Divine One, help us return to Creation.

Born of Earth, we can live nowhere else. We are the latest blossom of your enchantingly beautiful, infinitely mysterious, love-drenched creativity – the 14-billion-year evolution of yourself – and our home is here. Can a fish live out of water? Can a bird fly with no air? Can humans survive the cold toxic radiation of space? Desperate plans, false solutions, more foolishness.

But what can we do? Divine One, what do you need from us? Even as we ask, words burst from the depths of sacred consciousness:

"Be still. Be silent. Stop talking. Turn off TV and cell phone. Go outside. Open wide your eyes. I shine before you as Creation: vibrant, colorful, alive; the symphony of your life and destiny. Look intensely. Look without thought. Open your senses: seasons of Earth, power of wind, greenness of plant, wetness of rain, warmth of sun, smell of soil, abundance of life, chatter of bird and squirrel, busyness of ant and worm, darkness of night, love-making everywhere, all rising in the holiness of Creation. You don't have to figure this out because you are Creation. Let the one you were born to be take you home. Creation will heal you, then your tenderness, joy, and adoration will heal Creation."

May the Earth bless and keep us,
May truth lead the way,
May the ancestors see our efforts,
May peace finally stay.

May the heart inform our journey,
May Creation bring us home,
May our lives be deeply planted,
And may we know we're not alone.

May you find your way home with grace and love. John

Author Biography

John Robinson is a clinical psychologist with a second doctorate in ministry, an ordained interfaith minister, the author of ten books and numerous articles on the psychology, spirituality and mysticism of the new aging and the role of mystical activism in the climate crisis, and a frequent speaker on Conscious Aging across the country. You can learn more about his work at www. johnrobinson.org.

Source Material: A Brief Summary of My Work

I have been following a singular mystical vision for over twenty years. All my work – ten books, numerous articles, book chapters, blogs, interviews, classes, lectures and conference presentations – embodies and arises from this timeless and unchanging realization. What is this original revelation? It is the direct experience of the world as divine in substance, form and consciousness. It's all God! Literally. Not the anthropomorphic God created by humans in their likeness, but a living, divine and conscious universe of infinite beauty, love, and flow that we can learn to experience directly.

And it's all based on mysticism – the firsthand experience of the sacred – which was humanity's original religion. Upon its central revelations were built numerous world theologies shaped by culture, era, geography and personality, each one a prism refracting the original pantheistic vision into conceptual belief systems. If we want to understand the divine, and particularly if we wish to transform our current human crisis, we must return to the mystical consciousness of the divine world, an experience that becomes increasingly available in sacred aging. Here is a brief tour through my work.

Death of a Hero, Birth of the Soul: Answering the Call of Midlife (1995, 1997)

- The seminal vision for all my work
- Examines the male midlife passage
- Describes of the psychological, spiritual and mystical dimensions of the second half of life
- Introduces to the mystical experience – our original awareness of a living divine reality that underlies all religion
- Imagines the mystical transformations possible in the second half of life

But Where Is God? Psychotherapy and the Religious Search (1999)

- Conventional psychotherapy completely misses mystical dimension of healing
- This book for counseling professionals outlines the responsible integration of psychotherapy and spirituality
- Presents a profound model of the religious psyche and its spiritual journey

Ordinary Enlightenment: Experiencing God's Presence in Everyday Life (2000)

- Explores the experience of Presence central to the mystical experience: What it is, how can we experience it, and the many ways it transforms our perception of the world
- Introduces the practice of Mystical Consciousness awakening the awareness of God's Presence and the perception of Heaven on Earth

Finding Heaven Here (2009)

- My Doctor of Ministry dissertation
- Engages a chorus of mystic voices all describing the direct perception of the Heaven on Earth here and now.

- The earlier model of the religious psyche now evolves into a tool for understanding, perceiving, and living in Heaven on Earth (Heaven's Compass)
- Contains exercises for cultivating the mystical experience of Heaven on Earth

The Three Secrets of Aging (2012)

- Shares my own mystical experience of aging
- Describes the natural unfolding of mystical consciousness in the aging process
- Outlines the central dynamics of mystical aging: Aging is an initiation into a new dimension of life, a transformation of self and consciousness, and a revelation of a sacred world all around us.

Bedtime Stories for Elders: What Fairy Tales Can Teach Us About the New Aging (2012)

- Presents the mystical nature of aging in a fun and symbolic way
- A collection old and new fairy tales, each an allegory of the transformative dynamics of humanity's new aging.
- Journaling questions and experiential exercises help readers discover the meaning of these tales in their own lives.

What Aging Men Want: The Odyssey as a Parable of Male Aging (2013)

- Introduces The Odyssey as a profound myth of male aging (as Bly's Iron John did for midlife men)
- Men grow tired of the patriarchal model of compulsive warrior as they age.
- They long to come home to peace, quiet and love, but it's not easy after a lifetime of warrior competition.
- Odysseus' adventures on his ten-year journey home

symbolize the tasks men face in opening their hearts and coming home from the war.

Breakthrough **(2014)**

- Autobiographical novel about a middle-aged psychologist whose life is turned upside down through the mystical experiences of a new client.
- Increasingly affected by this client's altered state of consciousness, the psychologist journeys into the realm of divine consciousness and the revolutionary spirituality of aging, revealing possibilities never before imagined.

The Divine Human **(2016)**

- Culminates the journey into mystical aging
- Draws again on the words of the great mystics to describe the coming of a Divine Human in a Divine World.
- Adds my own mystical realizations, exercises for experiencing our personal divinity, and the possibilities of sacred action in healing the world.
- It lifts the veil on a new kind of humanity and new era of spiritual evolution.

Mystical Activism: Transforming a World in Crisis (2018)

- Transforms our activism by awakening the perception of sacred reality, which is powerfully motivating – we care for what we love and hold sacred
- Provides revolutionary new tools for "solving" problems in mystical consciousness
- Rekindles our relationship with soul and ancestors for their help
- Allows us to communicate with Creation herself to find out what she really needs

A Message to the Reader

Thank you for purchasing *Resilience: Aging with Vision, Hope and Courage in a Time of Crisis.* I hope it inspired the vision, hope and courage promised and will continue to support you in the complicated years ahead. Feel free to add a book review at your favorite online site. If you have comments, questions or interest in my other books, please visit me my website at www. johnrobinson.org and know that we are all in this together.

Bibliography

Baring, Anne (2009). *The Birds Who Flew Beyond Time*. Great Britain: Archive Publishing.

TRANSFORMATION

Transform your life, transform your world – Changemakers
Books publishes for individuals committed to transforming their
lives and transforming the world. Our readers seek to become
positive, powerful agents of change. Changemakers Books
inform, inspire, and provide practical wisdom and skills to
empower us to write the next chapter of humanity's future.
If you have enjoyed this book, why not tell other readers by
posting a review on your preferred book site.

The *Resilience* Series

The Resilience Series is a collaborative effort by the authors
of Changemakers Books in response to the 2020 coronavirus
epidemic. Each concise volume offers expert advice and
practical exercises for mastering specific skills and abilities.
Our intention is that by strengthening your resilience, you can
better survive and even thrive in a time of crisis.

Resilience: Adapt and Plan for the New Abnormal of the COVID-19 Coronavirus Pandemic
by Gleb Tsipursky

COVID-19 has demonstrated clearly that businesses, nonprofits,
individuals, and governments are terrible at dealing effectively
with large-scale disasters that take the form of slow-moving train-
wrecks. Using cutting-edge research in cognitive neuroscience
and behavioral economics on dangerous judgment errors
(cognitive biases), this book first explains why we respond so
poorly to slow-moving, high-impact, and long-term crises. Next,
the book shares research-based strategies for how organizations
and individuals can adapt effectively to the new abnormal of
the COVID-19 pandemic and similar disasters. Finally, it shows
how to develop an effective strategic plan and make the best
major decisions in the context of the uncertainty and ambiguity
brought about by COVID-19 and other slow-moving large-
scale catastrophes. The author, a cognitive neuroscientist and
behavioral economist and CEO of the consulting, coaching, and
training firm Disaster Avoidance Experts, combines research-
based strategies with real-life stories from his business and
nonprofit clients as they adapt to the pandemic.

Resilience: Aging with Vision, Hope and Courage in a Time of Crisis
by John C. Robinson

This book is for those over 65 wrestling with fear, despair, insecurity, and loneliness in these frightening times. A blend of psychology, self-help, and spirituality, it's meant for all who hunger for facts, respect, compassion, and meaningful resources to light their path ahead. The 74-year old author's goal is to move readers from fear and paralysis to growth and engagement: "Acknowledging the inspiring resilience and wisdom of our hard-won maturity, I invite you on a personal journey of transformation and renewal into a new consciousness and a new world."

Resilience: Connecting with Nature in a Time of Crisis
by Melanie Choukas-Bradley

Nature is one of the best medicines for difficult times. An intimate awareness of the natural world, even within the city, can calm anxieties and help create healthy perspectives. This book will inspire and guide you as you deal with the current crisis, or any personal or worldly distress. The author is a naturalist and certified forest therapy guide who leads nature and forest bathing walks for many organizations in Washington, DC and the American West. Learn from her the Japanese art of "forest bathing": how to tune in to the beauty and wonder around you with all your senses, even if your current sphere is a tree outside the window or a wild backyard. Discover how you can become a backyard naturalist, learning about the trees, wildflowers, birds and animals near your home. Nature immersion during stressful times can bring comfort and joy as well as opportunities for personal growth, expanded vision and transformation.

Resilience: Going Within in a Time of Crisis
by P.T. Mistlberger

During a time of crisis, we are presented with something of a fork in the road; we either look within and examine ourselves, or engage in distractions and go back to sleep. This book is intended to be a companion for men and women dedicated to their inner journey. Written by the author of seven books and founder of several personal growth communities and esoteric schools, each chapter offers different paths for exploring your spiritual frontier: advanced meditation techniques, shadow work, conscious relating, dream work, solo retreats, and more. In traversing these challenging times, let this book be your guide.

Resilience: Grow Stronger in a Time of Crisis
by Linda Ferguson

Many of us have wondered how we would respond in the midst of a crisis. You hope that difficult times could bring out the best in you. Some become stronger, more resilient and more innovative under pressure. You hope that you will too. But you are afraid that crisis may bring out your anxiety, your fears and your weakest communication. No one knows when the crisis will pass and things will get better. That's out of your hands. But *you* can get better. All it takes is an understanding of how human beings function at their best, the willpower to make small changes in perception and behavior, and a vision of a future that is better than today. In the pages of this book, you will learn to create the conditions that allow your best self to show up and make a difference - for you and for others.

Resilience: Handling Anxiety in a Time of Crisis
by George Hofmann

It's a challenging time for people who experience anxiety, and even people who usually don't experience it are finding their moods are getting the better of them. Anxiety hits hard and its symptoms are unmistakable, but sometimes in the rush and confusion of uncertainty we miss those symptoms until it's too late. When things seem to be coming undone, it's still possible to recognize the onset of anxiety and act to prevent the worst of it. The simple steps taught in this book can help you overcome the turmoil.

Resilience: The Life-Saving Skill of Story
by Michelle Auerbach

Storytelling covers every skill we need in a crisis. We need to share information about how to be safe, about how to live together, about what to do and not do. We need to talk about what is going on in ways that keep us from freaking out. We need to change our behavior as a human race to save each other and ourselves. We need to imagine a possible future different from the present and work on how to get there. And we need to do it all without falling apart. This book will help people in any field and any walk of life to become better storytellers and immediately unleash the power to teach, learn, change, soothe, and create community to activate ourselves and the people around us.

Resilience: Navigating Loss in a Time of Crisis
by Jules De Vitto

This book explores the many forms of loss that can happen in times of crisis. These losses can range from loss of business, financial security, routine, structure to the deeper losses of meaning, purpose or identity. The author draws on her background in transpersonal psychology, integrating spiritual insights and mindfulness practices to take the reader on a journey in which to help them navigate the stages of uncertainty that follow loss. The book provides several practical activities, guided visualization and meditations to cultivate greater resilience, courage and strength and also explores the potential to find greater meaning and purpose through times of crisis.

Resilience: Virtually Speaking
Communicating When you can't Meet Face to Face
by Teresa Erickson and Tim Ward

To adapt to a world where you can't meet face to face - with air travel and conferences cancelled, teams working from home - leaders, experts, managers and professionals all need to master the skills of virtual communication. Written by the authors of *The Master Communicator's Handbook*, this book tells you how to create impact with your on-screen presence, use powerful language to motivate listening, and design compelling visuals. You will also learn techniques to prevent your audience from losing attention, to keep them engaged from start to finish, and to create a lasting impact.

Resilience: Virtual Teams
Holding the Centre when you can't Meet Face-to-Face
by Carlos Valdes-Dapena

In the face of the COVID-19 virus organizations large and small are shuttering offices and factories, requiring as much work as possible be done from peoples' homes. The book draws on the insights of the author's earlier book, *Lessons from Mars*, providing a set of the powerful tools and exercises developed within the

Mars Corporation to create high performance teams. These tools have been adapted for teams suddenly forced to work apart, in many cases for the first time. These simple secrets and tested techniques have been used by thousands of teams who know that creating a foundation of team identity and shared meaning makes them resilient, even in a time of crisis.